THE PITTSBURGH THEOLOGICAL
MONOGRAPH SERIES

Dikran Y. Hadidian
General Editor

37

THE PATH TO TRANSCENDENCE

From Philosophy to Mysticism in Saint Augustine

The Path to TRANSCENDENCE

From Philosophy to Mysticism in Saint Augustine

by
Paul Henry

Introduction and translation
by
Francis F. Burch

The Pickwick Press
Pittsburgh, Pennsylvania
1981

Originally published as *La Vision d'Ostie: Sa place dans la vie et l'oeuvre de Saint Augustin*. Copyright© 1938. Editions J. Vrin. An early version of Chapter VII appeared as "Philosophy and Mysticism" in *The Downside Review* 79 (1961) pp. 297-316.

Library of Congress Cataloging in Publication Data

Henry, Paul, 1906-
The path to transcendence.

(The Pittsburgh theological monograph series; 37)

Translation of: La vision d'Ostie.

1. Augustine, Saint, Bishop of Hippo.
2. Ostia (Italy)—Miscellanea. I. Title.
II. Series.

BR1720.A9H3813 189'.2 81-23510
ISBN 0-915138-49-2 AACR2

THE PICKWICK PRESS
Pittsburgh, Pa.

This translation is dedicated

to

Tad, Julie and Meg

CONTENTS

INTRODUCTION

An English version of this essay should attract a variety of readers. It is a *locus classicus* for those interested in the life and thought of St. Augustine. It is the most comprehensive analysis of the vision at Ostia, one of the most significant passages in the *Confessions*, surely the most read of Augustine's works. It is a sensitive meditation on the process of mystical ascent, outlined in the vision at Ostia, which became the dominant pattern upon which Christian tradition has depended for its explanation and practice of religious life--from conversion to mystical union with God--since at least the fifth century.

At Ostia, therefore, an event occurred which transformed Augustine and ultimately the Church. Together with Monica, his mother, he experienced a moment of understanding, the thrill of beatitude. Years later he would struggle with language in the impossible task of trying to express these perceptions of the divine which surpass senses, intellect, and surely words. But at ease with the Neoplatonic pattern of contemplation, with the Neoplatonic description of the ascent of the soul, Augustine was convinced that Neoplatonism had helped him to God. If he adjusted the thought of Plotinus in subtle ways, he did so because he understood him more profoundly in the light of his own ecstasy and because Plotinus does, in fact, confess in his treatise *On the Beautiful* that his words are inadequate for communication of his transcendent experience, that ultimately only the experience itself can be the basis for mutual understanding. Plotinus had thus thrown down an implicit challenge to any writer who would grapple with the same subject and Augustine accepted.

Augustine knew that his experience at Ostia was also but roughly captured in his brief account and he would not have dared to maintain that the grace of God was bound by his psychology or the Neoplatonic pattern. Yet the history of western spirituality gives eloquent witness to the fact that he has spoken convincingly to mute inglorious mystics and that no one has given any other description which has gained wider acceptance or has been felt more consonant with the general experience of mankind in its progression toward and union with God. As even many of his critics admit, unhappily, to understand the vision at Ostia is to understand the central thrust of Christian spirituality in the West.

A few observations might be helpful, however, before we come to Paul Henry's essay. This work has provoked comment and stimulated research, while its principal thesis has withstood attack and remains sound. The durability is due in part to Henry's foresight. In the third chapter, he lists previous interpretations which vary from his own and thus anticipates the criticisms which are still advanced. Such opinions result from different and frequently justifiable interpretations of texts, and from unequal emphasis on incomplete biographical data, but most importantly from different theological presuppositions. Nevertheless, some precisions and qualifications should be offered which take into account the advances in Neoplatonic and Augustinian scholarship (many made by Henry himself), flesh out a few sketchy sections, and shift emphasis here and there. Commenting on such progress, Henry recently expressed particular admiration for Pierre Courcelle's extended and profound treatment of the central problems posed by the Vision at Ostia in *Lettres grecques en Occident* (Paris, 1943), translated by Harry E. Wedeck as *Late Latin Writers and*

Their Greek Sources (Cambridge, 1969).

As in most other literary controversies, any discussion of the vision at Ostia must concern a number of possibilities and probabilities. The reader will ultimately be attracted to one interpretation rather than another, because it appears to offer the most coherent analysis of the whole passage, or because it appears to make the best account of all important details, or perhaps it appears to illuminate more fully the significance of the text in the context of the author's life and works. To the translator's continuing admiration, Henry's essay continues to do all three.

Style

Literary style is more than mere verbal facility: it is both a point of view and a consequent mode of expression, and develops as an author feeds on successive materials. Like the lion, the writer is made from assimilated lambs. He is not always conscious of what nourished him, where it was assimilated, and how much of it remains vital. Thus the evolving styles of theologians, even of Fathers and Doctors of the Church, can be important and can reveal a sequence of influences which may color our interpretations and nuance our judgments.

For centuries, readers of Augustine have been conscious of the echoes of his works down through the ages, but only recently, after prolonged research and minute comparisons of texts, has it been possible to begin to hear in his writings echoes of what went before him. Some of his passages are filled with allusions, paraphrases, catch phrases, borrowed terms, borrowed structures; for Augustine did not share the modern passion for originality. The legacies of the past, Christian or otherwise, were preserved to be used. He found no disgrace in being a disciple of Cicero, Plotinus, Christ, and at least some of his audience would have caught reverberations from the past, the weight of tradition, the wisdom of God and man. But the process of stylistic evolution begins in infancy.

Robert Frost once quipped: "Parents send their children to school when it is already too late to teach them anything." A Freudian exaggeration, this remark still stresses what much Augustinian scholarship has tended to forget. Before there was schooling, there was childhood: a religious ambience preceded Augustine's formal education. He grew up in a milieu of belief and from infancy absorbed scriptural language and Christian ideas. These resources would not be explicitly exploited until later, but his exposure to Christianity constitutes his earliest encounter with a distinctive point of view which was comprehensive enough to be a system of thought, and with a mode of expression subtle enough to express it in a plan of life. This fact should not be forgotten when we consider Augustine the "pagan" who did not "understand" the scriptures. And Monica acts as a constant reminder of his Christian childhood. She continues to feed her son, to propose concepts, principles, and passages which the liberated and sophisticated Augustine found simplistic and was trying his best to avoid.

The young rhetorician and philosopher was further formed through assimilation of the great classics of thought and expression. There was imitation of models, practice of techniques, exercise in adjusting knowledge and language to various audiences, and the honing of phrases to philosophic precision. With time, some skills of inquiry and expression became second nature. Literary originality and insight were to come later.

After his conversion, Augustine was both an apologist and a theologian. He was interested in swaying his audience (no one would accuse even the mature bishop of forgetting his rhetoric), but he was more concerned about accurate formulations of Christian doctrine. Quite simply, Augustine devoted his rhetorical and philosophical skills to the religion of his childhood. Apologist, he was a Christian rhetorician. Theologian, he was a lover of wisdom in quest of that eternal wisdom which is the all-knowing Father, incarnate wisdom which is the revealing Son, saving wisdom which is the indwelling Spirit.

The importance of Augustine's earliest verbal and intellectual experience has sometimes been overlooked. Comparing Augustine with Marius Victorinus, an important figure who will be mentioned later, Etienne Gilson remarks: "Augustine seems much less concerned with introducing Neoplatonism into Christian theology than with limiting its invasion. The theology of Victorinus shows what would have happened if the genius of Augustine had not kept Neoplatonism within the strict limits of Christian faith" (*History of Christian Philosophy in the Middle Ages*, 1955, p. 67). But Gilson ignores the fact that the rhetorician Victorinus did not convert to Christianity until old age--his seventies, it is generally believed--after a lifetime absorbing pagan authors. It would be remarkable if the influence of such writers were not more prominent in Victorinus than in Augustine. One had to examine Christianity in the light of lifelong paganism; the other admits that he restlessly scrutinized paganism in the light of childhood Christianity. This is not so much a matter of "genius," as Gilson would have it, but an ingrained way of seeing and saying. It is a question of style.

Historicity

Is the account of the vision at Ostia accurate? In need of an episode to bring the life of his mother to a climax, perhaps the author simply invented a scene and the vision never occurred. Such a charge has been made against other passages in the *Confessions* and the *dramatic fiction* is admittedly a common rhetorical device. But if we are unwilling to go to this extreme, still we cannot "prove" that every word was spoken nor establish with minute precision the authenticity of the recorded sequence of phrases and events.

Augustine seems to have foreseen such objections. He tells us that something did happen at Ostia; he then warns us that the reported conversation is only an approximation. We know from experience that recollections are in some ways reconstructions, that imagination is selective and can supply for faulty memory, that stories improve with telling. But Augustine's remark should not be viewed as apologetic, nor his creative imagination as an inferior faculty. No novice writer, he knew exactly what he wanted to do and possessed the talent and technique to come very close to achieving it.

Recollection need not distort events, it need not alter the truth, it need not, in short, do any disservice to history. On the contrary, recollection is the unavoidable, internalization of events, and preserves what would otherwise be caught in space and washed away in time. In one form or another, all history is a re-collection, successive collecting, arranging, and rearranging of materials to achieve progressive clarity. At this late date, no serious historian or literary critic would reveal such insensitivity to Augustine's purpose and art by accusing him of sloppy reporting and distortion of the past.

Significance emerges with the selection and heightening of detail, and this process is achieved through new perspectives which come only with the passage of time. Significant experience does not always reveal much of its significance on the spot. In retrospect, some events reveal an influence which could not have been predicted; others have not lived up to expectation. At different times, different things appear more or less important to different people and our natural curiosity is rarely satisfied with chronologies of external fact: we are interested in insight into facts, the significance of events, the viewpoints of others, and the vibrancy of their narratives. The great autobiographer tries to satisfy these tastes, struggles to place the elements of his life in perspective, and to make the dead past live.

In the process of literary composition, did Augustine read out of his experience or into it? And is such a question either answerable or important? If the past illumines the present, the present illumines the past, and psychological realism is an unavoidable phenomenon; for the interior present is surely as real as the exterior past. Much reflection may have been required to discover the significance of the event at Ostia and Augustine may have experimented considerably before he achieved a satisfactory structure and language for communicating such significance. But what is certain is that he could not have realized at the time of the event what the experience would mean to him as the years went by, and what he wishes to give us in the *Confessions* is more than the external event from the past. Augustine shares the internalized event which has assumed an importance proportionate to its increasing influence and which has revealed further meaning in enlarging perspectives. A "replay" of the ecstasy would have been an impoverished account. From the vantage point of mature years, Augustine the bishop saw the vision at Ostia as the high point of his mother's life, a turning point in his own, and an ideal for anyone in quest of God.

Literary Innovation

Great writers contribute something of substance or develop forms or evolve techniques: they advance the tradition. As T. S. Eliot puts it, the creative writer "takes the next step." Augustine took several steps, but in the *Confessions* most particularly we are present at an extraordinary moment in the evolution of Christian literature.

St. Augustine was not the first to write about Christian life nor the first Christian to experience mystical elevation and liberation, but he was the first to synthesize earlier traditions, literary and religious, with such brilliance, that the story of his life is recognized among the greatest achievements of western thought. St. Athanasius had written what is generally called the first Christian biography, his *Life of Saint Antony*. Using for his model the pagan encomium of the wise man, he adapted it to suit the life of a saint. St. Jerome's *De viris illustribus* is a collection of simple sketches of edifying lives. In both works we learn *what* such figures did for God and neighbor and *why*, but we do not really learn *how*. We are external observers, "by their fruits" we know them, but we do not get inside.

With the *Confessions*, the account of Augustine's conversion, Christian autobiography comes of age. Aware of how the tradition of the encomium, whether of hero or seer, was committed to external narration, he adapts the form to meet the needs of internal narrative and produces a psychology in its most literal sense--the study of a soul. Through Augustine's life we discover not only the *what* and the *why*, but also the *how*. Perhaps only in an *auto*biography, and in an extraordinary one at that, can we witness the stages of human cooperation with transforming grace. In the *Confessions* we are so privileged and discover a method for ascent to God throughout life and, more precisely, in that microcosm of perfect Christian life, a moment of perfect prayer.

Augustine's *Confessions* are written as if to answer the plea: "Teach us to transcend!" He knew from experience that motive and goal mean little without a practical plan of action. We too have known from childhood that even mice cannot bell cats without method. The best he could do was to offer examples of how God had worked on him and with him, and how he had cooperated with God. In humility he presents himself as model and opens his life to reveal method. But if his life reveals a method, it does so because Augustine had struggled with the systems of the past, had tried various ways of life and ways to God, had pitted one experience against another. Ultimately it was Christian Neoplatonism that won the day.

Christian Neoplatonism

Neoplatonism was not an esoteric doctrine during the life of Augustine (354-430): key terms and central principles were in the air. How many of the treatises of Plotinus (204-270) were available and whether in Latin translation or the Greek original is the subject of some speculation. But important ideas never remain confined to their texts and the indirect influence of Plotinus through his disciples and commentators, whether Christian or not, is evident.

The influence of St. Antony (250-356) upon Augustine, long thought to be purely Christian, is not without Neoplatonic elements. Athanasius' *Life* of the Egyptian monk contains too many parallels with Porphyry's encomium of Plotinus for the similarity to be accidental. Moreover, Antony himself spent time in Alexandria, where Plotinus had studied under the alleged former Christian, Ammonius Saccas, and with the two Origens, one of whom was to become a celebrated Christian theologian. Such was Antony's reputation for wisdom that two Neoplatonic philosophers sought him out at his hermitage. They "admired" and "embraced" him; for the father of monasticism was unschooled in their philosophy, but--and this is surely Athanasius' point in recounting this meeting--not incompatible with Neoplatonists, as with the Arians. He had found a way of life, a method for purification and illumination, which had something to teach even these advanced disciples of wisdom. It is hard to believe that this point would have been lost on Augustine.

Athanasius seems to soften Antony's resistance to worldly learning and Augustine will not follow the precise example of Antony. The parallel between Antony and Monica could not be more obvious. Both give witness to a wisdom higher than that of intellectualistic philosophies and insist that the path to transcendence goes beyond the mind. But the same parallel does not exist between Antony and Augustine. Antony had found school unpleasant; Augustine was so impassioned with learning and had developed so keen a mind and such exceptional powers of expression that it was too late for him to turn his back on the intellectual life and retire to the desert. Nor did the faith demand such a retreat. Whatever else the Church would require of him, it did not ask renunciation of intelligence. It would concur that human intelligence must search for the Way, the Truth, and the Life, but would caution that wisdom is a gift and mystical union with the Infinite a rare and special grace.

When compared with the biography of Antony, Augustine's autobiography is very intellectual. Augustine is full of praise for Antony and Monica and aware that they raised their minds and hearts to God without rhetoric, philosophy, and even much speculative theology, but he recognizes the value of the mind in the quest for God and knows that human intelligence is part of the "fullness we have all received."

The role of the convert Marius Victorinus (275-?) is here important. What Victorinus gave the Church was more than the witness of a famous and intelligent man who embraced the faith toward the end of his long life. He also wrote the first Latin commentaries on scripture and used Neoplatonism as a basis for extended theological speculation. His considerations of the Trinity in particular foreshadow Augustine's. For Augustine, Victorinus represented intelligence at the service of the Church, creative use of human achievement to explain divine revelation, the search for theological method and structure. Jerome was not oblivious of what Victorinus had done and criticized the books of his *Adversus Arium* for being "quite obscure" and composed "in a dialectical fashion," rather than according to the more traditional scriptural or rhetorical modes. Augustine obviously did not share Jerome's bias. The "new" theology gave promise, he was going to explore it, and he was not alone.

The sermons of Ambrose, for example *De bono mortis* and *De Isaac*, offered Augustine not only fine rhetoric, but also Christian doctrine explained with the help of Neoplatonism (Pierre Courcelle, *Recherches sur les Confessions de Saint Augustin*, Paris, 1950, p. 138). Ambrose was not a figure from the past, but a respected, intelligent, forward-looking bishop who used Neoplatonism effectively in his preaching.

Athanasius, Antony, Victorinus, Ambrose--Augustine was not the first to appreciate and exploit Neoplatonism for Christian enlightenment. He did not have to search it out or justify his enthusiasm. For Augustine, Christian Neoplatonism was simply a fact of intellectual life.

Monasticism

Like Existentialism in the middle of this century, Neoplatonism in Augustine's time was compatible with a variety of beliefs. If there are common elements in the atheist Jean-Paul Sartre, the Jew Martin Buber, the Protestant Karl Jaspers, and the Catholic Gabriel Marcel, nevertheless these thinkers do not always understand and apply terms and principles in the same way. What we come to identify as a literary, philosophical, or theological movement has been precisely that, a movement, and movement is an indication of life, growth, change. A school may spring up to preserve traditional definitions and interpretations, but the veneration of followers is not the vitality of the masters. The Christian Neoplatonists worked in the heat of enthusiasm, before Neoplatonic philosophy had cooled, and they molded meaning to suit their needs.

Neoplatonism in Augustine's time, like Existentialism in our own, may be encountered in unexpected places; for popular philosophies characteristically influence the thought and language of many who never bother to read the philosophers. But popular philosophies are never popular merely because they feed the intellect: their appeal lies principally in the fact that they offer a plan of action or way of life.

Peter Brown notes: "The exhortation to love 'Wisdom' had always been couched in strongly religious terms. It is not surprising that by the fourth century, it had come to act as the bridgehead in traditional culture both for the idea of religious conversion, and even of a conversion to monastic life" (*Augustine of Hippo,* Berkeley, 1969, pp. 40-41). Not surprisingly, the lovers of wisdom vied with one another in their research for the perfect way to wisdom. The apparent failure of so many philosophers to attain this goal, indicates that desire, enthusiasm, good will, and even a knowledge of philosophy are not sufficient. Method is crucial. It not only distinguishes one philosophy from another; it is purported to be the way to understanding and the path to union with wisdom. But how many ways of understanding are there? How many ways to wisdom? Monastic life offered a favorable environment for the quest.

Monasticism, like Neoplatonism, was in the air. Athanasius' *Life of Antony* was a "best seller" and a forerunner of monastic "rules." Numerous monasteries had been established in the east and the enthusiasm had recently spread to the west. Yet Augustine and others did not feel called to the desert. A different model was needed. And so as there was a quest for method in the process of conversion, in the dialectic of mystical ascent, in the patterns of theological commentary and speculation, so too there was quest for a rule of daily, Christian life. The monasteries became more intellectual, more open. The academies and symposiums of antiquity were imitated in Christian communities of love which drew their members away from the distractions of the world to devote their lives to the study and worship of the things of God, but they remained less distant from the world, and especially the world of the intellect, than Antony's monks.

Augustine was familiar with Ambrose's monastic institutions at Milan and as bishop would draw his own priests around him into community. The former rhetorician was still a teacher, but decidedly more pastoral and intellectual than Antony. Yet like Antony, Augustine doubtlessly considered monastic life the epitome of Christian existence, in the sense that it represented the total giving of the self to God, a life striving to transcend the merely human, methodical growth in intimacy with God. He certainly considered mystical experience, momentary contact with God beyond space and time, the epitome of monastic and hence Christian life. This pattern is important. Such convictions have left a heavy print on Christian spirituality and have provoked periodic outcries that a spirituality which is more activist, more neighborly, more socially and politically involved is more in harmony with the Gospels.

The so-called "Rule of Augustine," as we know it, may not have been in the hands of Augustine's monastic contemporaries, but it bears witness to the fact that Augustine was remembered as one of the founders and theoreticians of western monasticism. His theory is capsulized in the vision at Ostia; it is Neoplatonic.

The importance of Neoplatonism in western spirituality can scarcely be exaggerated and even David Knowles, who regrets it, acknowledges the influence: "As a consequence of this 'contamination' it became (and still remains) very difficult when examining spiritual writers of all centuries to dissever the traditional Christian teaching and the experiential wisdom of the Church from the doctrines, which may or may not be viable in a Christian context, of a wholly non-Christian system of thought. While the gain to mystical theology from the ideas and methods of the most spiritual and theistic of all ancient thinkers is undoubted, the accretion to Catholic spiritual theology of purely speculative propositions and techniques has brought with it confusion and problems not a few" (*The Nature of Mysticism,* 1966, pp. 111-112).

In all fairness to Plotinus, his treatise *On the Beautiful,* for all its "speculative propositions," does recount a profound experience which some have called mystical. But how can we measure what is Christian or non-Christian in such a context? Where is the line to be drawn between the human and the divine? The question of theological method, debated in Augustine's time, remains a subject of dispute among his commentators.

Theological Method

Once the secular has been separated from the sacral in Augustine's sources, the specter which haunts all theology appears. Reliance on scripture alone allows an hermetic system, a fixed arcanum. But a heavy part of Christianity has accepted some form of tradition. Development of doctrine is thought possible.

Now the evolution of doctrine involved the subtle interrelation of revelation and the successive ways in which it is explained. If the form as well as the content of scripture is not independent of the Divine Author, and if inspiration is somehow responsible for the choice and disposition of biblical elements, still the form or structure or methodology of a theology has not the warrant of revelation, no guarantee of inspiration, and certainly no automatic link with the sustaining life of Christian tradition. Some theologies are short-lived; others prosper and may produce a generation or two of committed students; a very few attract such a following and are perceived as so closely associated with the faith that they draw life from the revelation they continue to illuminate and impart this life to the Christian community which is drawn to them.

Only the most presumptuous theologian would dare to affirm that God speaks through him, because he knows that theology, as any other human study, is open to fads and that libraries are crammed with outdated theological works, some of which once enjoyed great popularity. But somehow, through the interplay of various explanations or revelation and through the response of the Christian community, tradition thrives. With time a select number of works emerges as having made some genuine contribution to the tradition; even a smaller number continue over the years to advance the tradition and to nourish the faithful. The rare theologian produces a classic work, one which continues to be a source of grace and through which God appears to speak to his people. Augustine is such a theologian and the *Confessions* are such a work.

Nevertheless, the relation of human form and divine content poses particular problems. Theologies derive their methodologies and structures from other disciplines, literary, historical, archeological, psychological, sociological, philosophical. Is a methodology specific to theology possible or necessary? God continues to act and to reveal Himself in His creation, which some Fathers of the Church have called the "second book of revelation": through advancing skills of inquiry, growing understanding, and repeated experience, the human mind continues to explore the world and self, and to clarify opaque passages of the word of God. These advances are not independent. Why should anyone regret that God's work, specifically the mind of man, should be brought to bear upon His word and work? To what degree is what God has made unholy? To what degree is what Christ redeemed un-Christian? To what degree does the limited perspective and expression of any human understanding distort the divine message?

Augustine is obviously indebted to secular material and this debt has raised some of the above questions. Is he more Neoplatonic than Christian, more philosophical than theological, more intellectual than mystical? Pierre Courcelle discussed the state of the question (*Recherches*, pp. 11 and 222-26) some twenty years ago. Unanimity has not yet arisen.

Was Augustine more of a Neoplatonist than a Christian? If this question cannot be answered, it can at least be seen in perspective. Development of doctrine is situated in time and space: not every element of revelation appears always and everywhere of equal importance, and the elucidation of the deposit of faith depends not only upon grace and the native quality and inclination of the questioning mind, but also upon the variety and subtlety of the intellectual tools available. In short, development of doctrine depends upon the training of the theologian, a training always subject to the influences, pressures, events, and perhaps especially to what is in intellectual vogue. Augustine was no exception.

We can make a similar charge against Thomas Aquinas whose Aristotelianism is more obvious than Augustine's Neoplatonism. Was Teilhard de Chardin too inspired by the Darwinians? Was John Courtney Murray seduced by the American political experiment? Not to mention a rash of recent authors who would christianize Hegel and Marx and even Fidel Castro. The theologies of evolution, do they represent a betrayal of the faith, an enrichment of Christianity, a development of the very tradition to which some would oppose them?

Was Augustine more of a philosopher than a theologian?

He appreciated the part that the tools of the intellect have to play in the illumination of revelation, in the development of doctrine. Human difficulties in the face of revelation have involved essentially problems of perceptivity, a perceptivity which evolves in each and through the ages, so that in some ways humanity's approach to revelation is progressively more sophisticated. Truth is indivisible: any advance in any way of knowing, any discovery of something new, any clarification of perceptions, any sharpening of human faculties either aids comprehension or is actual understanding, direct or oblique, of God's word or work. Thus all true understanding is an approach to God; a contribution to human understanding is participation in God's revealing and thus redemptive work; and it is a function of the Christian teacher to hand on and to advance the tradition which perpetuates these evolutions, to lead the Church militant one step further in understanding God's revelation, to "take the next step" toward the Trinity. The object of theology is Divine, but our minds and mental tools are very human.

Was Augustine more intellectual than mystical? We have grown up with the traditional and convenient distinction between the "purgative, illuminative, and unitive ways," but we should not consider these "stages" of spiritual growth as necessarily incompatible or mutually exclusive. What is distinguishable, is not always distinct. God need not be so inhibited. Augustine's "moment of understanding" at Ostia was a moment of union and a moment of love. In human relationships with the Divine, what need be simultaneous and what successive? Masters of the spiritual life have hoped that their methodical descriptions might help us to dispose ourselves for cooperation with the action of grace, but they only wish to lead us to a point where we transcend the stages of their method; for ultimately union with the Transcendent will transcend human constructs.

Thus the methodologies of spirituality, and indeed all theologies, are not to be confused with revelation or the Sacraments or the Church or mystical experience, they are not to be confused with "God with us". The Church has been careful not to equate theology and dogma. The only warrant which Augustine advances for his method is his belief that it worked for him and he reveals it in the hope that it may work for others. Centuries later, in the apophatic tradition of Plotinus and Augustine, Aquinas would remark that there are certain things beyond our understanding and expression, that we learn about them only through experience. *Facientes cognoscant*. Today we are still in quest of the ineffable and still looking for a more efficient method.

Transcendental Meditation

Pursuit of the transcendent experience is not new. It has been pursued in Hebrew poetry (the *Fourth Psalm*), in the Greek philosophic tradition (the *Enneads* of Plotinus), in Roman rhetoric (the *Hortensius* of Cicero), but Augustine pulled these three together to serve the needs of Christian mystical contemplation and formulated a pattern of ascent which has not ceased to serve the western world. The ancients would be disappointed by what currently passes for transcendental experience. Transcendental Meditation is neither philosophical nor religious, it will not lead to the heights or depths beyond us. It will, of course, leave us with ourselves, if that will satisfy us. But great minds and hearts have never been content with self or peace with self or satisfaction in self, with a life without a quest for being or nothingness, without a Jesus or a Marx. But where is a satisfactory model for Transcendental Meditation?

The vision at Ostia may be said to be *the* western prototype of Christian Transcendental Meditation, as the *Confessions* may be said to contain *the* western prototype of Christian religious conversion. But although Augustine's autobiography is an ancient work, it is not a simple one and responds to our complex human aspirations. We thirst for life, but like Nietzsche, have a fascination with death; we envy the fullness of being, but are nihilistic enough to be drawn toward absolute nothingness; we have faith in the long-term promises of God our Father, but are children of Adam and weak before immediate delights; we are curious about the heights and have a Faustian wish to explore the depths. Jean-Paul Sartre would borrow Jean Wahl's distinction between "transascendance" and "transdescendance" to designate the tensions of the human condition. Augustine knew this condition well. He weighed his experiences, cooperated with grace, moved toward God, and his story is still exciting. It has good characters, a solid plot, imaginative imagery, rhetorical finesse, and just enough poetry to stir our emotions at just the right moment. Generations have put down this book moved and convinced by the author's conviction that God has made us for Himself, and our hearts are restless until they rest in Him. If "the style is the man," how full Augustine has appeared, by comparison with more literarily, philosophically, theologically, mystically--in a word humanly--limited commentators on the divine word and work.

Paul Henry's essay is really concerned with two profound experiences which mark decisive phases in Augustine's transcendence. The first experience, the contemplation at Milan (*Conf*. VII, 13-27), occurred as Augustine was comparing the philosophy of the Platonists, especially that of Plotinus, with the teaching of the scripture and tradition. The essential harmony of the two resolved his intellectual difficulties and allowed him to achieve a synthesis of faith and reason. The second experience, the vision at Ostia (*Conf*. IX, 23-26), occurred as Augustine and Monica were discussing the happiness of the blessed in heaven. In the course of their conversation, each experienced mystical contact with God. Augustine was allowed to break the hold of the world and the flesh, and turned the total affection of his will towards God. With the vision at Ostia, Augustine's conversion is fully achieved and the elements of faith, reason, and mysticism unite to form a new synthesis, "the fulness of faith" insofar as it is attainable in this life.

One caution should be made to the Anglo-Saxon reader who may be tempted to find Augustine's and Henry's texts overrich at times: metaphor is piled upon metaphor as they attempt to clarify the mystical process. It would be a mistake to rush past these images as annoying examples of Latin ornamentation. They are straining to communicate elusive mystical experience. Henri Bergson faces this problem squarely in his *Introduction to Metaphysics* and details the literary technique through which he hoped to lead his reader to a specific intuition. "No image will replace the intuition of duration, but many different images, taken from quite different orders of things, will be able, through the convergence of their action, to direct the consciousness to the precise point where there is an intuition to seize on. By choosing images as dissimilar as possible, any one of them will be prevented from usurping the place of the intuition it is instructed to call forth, since it would then be driven out immediately by its rivals. By seeing that in spite of their differences in aspect they all demand of our mind the same kind of attention and, as it were, the same degree of tension, one will gradually accustom the consciousness to a particular and definitely determined disposition, precisely the one it will have to adopt in order to appear unveiled to itself" (New York, 1946, p. 195).

The technique is not a new one. The New Testament contains over 80 different imaginative expressions for the Church. These images approach the ineffable reality through a wide range of similitudes with the commonplace, but do not describe the Church as it is in itself and, for all the insight they may bring, ultimately leave the mystery of the Church intact. Mystical experience must also be approached obliquely, through analogies; it cannot be described in itself. Henry uses traditional metaphors of mystical language, those of the senses--the journey, vision, touch, the banquet, the odor of sweetness--but he also plays with metaphors of science--the archaeological dig, organic growth, the fusion of elements, the electromagnetic interplay of forces. Clusters of metaphors may lack the directness and clarity of forthright prose, but there are some subjects which leave the writer--and apparently even the Divine Author and inspired writers--little choice among the limited tools of linguistic analysis and expression. The Transcendent remains transcendent.

The English versions of Plotinus and Augustine are the translator's own. Stephen MacKenna's rendition of the *Enneads* and Frank Sheed's version of the *Confessions* have been consulted, but for contextual reasons it has often seemed better to remain closer to permissible differences of interpretation contained in the translations employed by the author: Pierre de Labriolle's version of the *Confessions;* Emile Brehier's of the *Enneads*.

A word of gratitude for the Augustinian and Plotinian scholarship of the Rev. Frederick Homann, S.J., whose suggestions are always important, and of the Rev. Patrick Brannan, S.J., whose encouragement and assistance really constitute a collaboration, and to my Mother who read the introduction and made several valuable corrections.

"Buena Vista"
Leonardtown, Maryland
15 August 1980

CHAPTER ONE

The Summit

> Conloquebamur ergo soli valde dulciter et *praeterita obliviscentes in ea quae sunt ante extenti* quaerebamus inter nos. . . .
> (*Conf.*, IX, 23)

We are all familiar with Ary Scheffer's painting of the vision at Ostia.* Monica and Augustine are seated together lost in ecstasy. Augustine is in the foreground on a slightly lower plane. The white veils of the saintly widow stand in contrast to the somber toga of the young African rhetorician, symbols of their two lives: one utterly unperturbed and pure; the other harrowed by tribulations of soul and disturbed by violent passions. Augustine has returned to God; Monica has recovered her son. Her prayers have been answered and happiness radiates from her wan face. Yet the present peace still shows traces of previous struggles. Over these serene, handsome, medallion-like faces, the graving tool of suffering has passed and tears have flowed like acid.

Their hands are intertwined, an expression of their mutual love, and their glances, which meet in another world, reveal their common love of God. The entire vision at Ostia is

---

* Ary Scheffer painted at least four versions of this work: one is in the Louvre, one in the Tate Gallery, one in the Dordrecht Museum. (Translator's note).

summed up in these hands and glances. Moreover, the vision at Ostia was in itself the whole life of Monica and Augustine concentrated into a supreme moment. It was the summit towards which they had been climbing, towards which the mother had been helping her son, and it was here that they had to part: Monica because her task was accomplished; Augustine because his work was just beginning and because the Church was calling him. It was the turning point of Augustine's life; the climax of Monica's, a life which derived its meaning from her son's. From this peak we can survey the two phases of Augustine's momentous life: behind him stood the darkness of Mani and his disciples, scepticism, pride, and the flesh; before him lay solid ground, a land of cool shadows and dazzling light, of love and contemplation, and through this rich panorama of nature and grace winds a royal road which the convert was determined to follow with unwavering step.

No one questions the depth and extent of Augustine's influence upon Western thought, philosophy, and religion, or the key position of his conversion in his life, or of the *Confessions* among his works. In fact, we sometimes almost tend to think that he ceased to exist at baptism and wrote nothing worth reading after his autobiography. Thus it is most important to make a close study of the experience that marked the end of the most important phase of Augustine's growth, of the high point of the *Confessions*, the vision at Ostia. At this unique moment in Augustine's life and works, emerged the principal traits which would forever characterize his teachings: some were derived from ancient sources; others flowed from an original, basic inspiration. Brief as it may have been, this decisive moment was teeming with Augustine's whole past and future. Such a sudden and profound evolution, situated in space and time, is highly personal, and yet the conversion of Augustine and the ecstasy in which it was fully achieved have universal value: they move beyond the limits of history to take their place within the realm of religious philosophy and metaphysics. Psychological phenomena reveal general laws. Whether for peace or discord, this event marked the encounter of the individual and the race, mystical experience and organized religion, philosophy and history, paganism and Christianity, inspiring example and brilliant writing, tradition and reason. It was the convergence of all the interior and exterior forces that exerted an influence upon a milieu, a school, a person.

If we try to isolate each thread, we run the risk of ripping this picture by some clumsy and insensitive movement, but we must attempt analysis, if we wish to appreciate the rich complexity of the synthesis. The patient, prudent untying of a knot is the most effective means of understanding the workmanship involved in its tangles. Precisely because the neophyte's ecstasy was so filled with memories and so rich in promise, the depth of our understanding will depend upon our discovery of its sources in the convert's life and of their development throughout the bishop's works.

The separation of the constitutive elements of a living whole is surely something of a sacrilege, but it is a crime required by our mental limitations. However, the awkward result of this process can be partially repaired by combining it with another analytical procedure, one still inadequate but slightly better suited to the material. Once we have made a long, patient study of the fleeting experience of the vision at Ostia and have taken into account all the details, we should consider it from a variety of viewpoints. Viewpoint is crucial: it can be literary, psychological, historical, doctrinal, but it should allow us to grasp some fundamental aspect, something essential to the scene under consideration.

These successive studies should remain brief, proportionate to their object; they will never be able to rival its depth nor exhaust its richness.

*
*   *

Augustine had returned slowly and gradually to his childhood faith. The principal stages of his conversion are sufficiently well-known and need no detailing here. For some years he had been a staunch and fervent initiate of Manichaeism, yet he had been disturbed by difficulties which the most illustrious teachers of the sect had been unable to resolve. At this time he was attracted to the scepticism of the New Academy. He was thirty years old and taught rhetoric in Milan. Here, as he recounts in Books V and VI of the *Confessions*, he became acquainted with Ambrose, the illustrious bishop of the imperial city. The rhetorician was impressed by the bishop, but Ambrose was overburdened with work and difficult to meet. Monica, who had recommended the bishop to her son, continued to work more directly for his conversion. She urged him to marry rather than to continue living as he had been for the past fifteen years.

Book VII is concerned with a crucial period. One of Augustine's friends put into his hands "some books of the Platonists." The young disillusioned rhetorician was amazed: they were both a revelation and a liberation. He felt transported into a new interior world in which the sun, to speak as Plotinus, is God himself. The philosophical or mystical assent which followed this reading has justly been called the first "summit" of the *Confessions*. The starting signal had been given; hereafter events moved quickly. Augustine's inborn love of all that was noble and beautiful, and the deep attraction that was surely drawing him to God were going to lead him to the very heart of Christianity. *Amor meus, pondus meum.*

Book VIII contains an account of three authentic religious experiences. The first two are described to Augustine by friends; they are a preparation for and a decisive factor in his own conversion. The saintly old man Simplicianus, to whom Augustine had gone for advice and with whom he shared his enthusiasm for the Platonists, told him how Marius Victorinus, the translator of these works, had embraced the faith of the Gospels and had joined the Church at the very height of his career.

A short time later, Augustine encountered Ponticianus, a high court dignitary. While visiting Augustine and Alypius, his friend, Ponticianus chanced upon a copy of St. Paul's Epistles on the gaming table. He congratulated his hosts and turned the conversation to Antony, the Egyptian monk whose name was then well-known among Christians. He also told them about two of the Emperor's young officers at Trier. While they had been out walking one day, they had stumbled upon a *Life* of Antony in the hut of pious monks and, impressed by his example, decided to leave the world and to follow the life of the evangelical counsels. Augustine was disturbed by this story. When Ponticianus left, Augustine returned to the garden visibly shaken. As he lay stretched out under a fig tree, weeping with emotion, he heard the mysterious *Tolle lege* which he took for an invitation from heaven. He got up, returned to Alypius and opened the book of the Apostle at random. He came upon the text in the Epistle to the Romans which urges chastity in most vigorous terms. Augustine immediately recovered his peace. The tempest was far behind him. He was entering the port. He hurried to Monica and told her what had just happened. The eighth, the most moving book of the *Confessions*, is brought to a close with the joy of his saintly mother.

Book IX shows us the convert in retirement at Cassiciacum chatting with some friends on philosophical and other questions. The *Dialogues* composed at this time were written *tamquam in pausatione*. It was a resting place. Before climbing to the third and final summit of his religious experiences, he paused for breath. His works, he tells us, already served Christ--many critics have denied this--but they still showed the effects of a rhetorician's (*Conf.*, IX, 7) and, we might add, a metaphysician's pride. For he was quite willing to draw inspiration from the Neoplatonists whom he openly admired. At Cassiciacum, Augustine was as much a Christian as he was a philosopher: if he read the *Enneads*, he also recited the Psalms in prayer. But he was a Christian at heart and not in fact. Even though he had already promised himself totally to the service of the Church, his being was not yet marked with the seal of Christ. He still lacked the *signaculum* of baptism. He therefore wrote to Ambrose that he might share with him his desires and feelings, and, on the 24th of April in the year 387, about six months after the scene in the garden, he received at the hands of the bishop of Milan the sacrament that made him a Christian in body and in soul, for time and for eternity.

Converts whose souls are as sensitive and as profound as Augustine's--John Henry Newman comes to mind--do not, as a rule, experience any new intense emotion upon their earnestly desired, but long-delayed entrance into the Church. Had this been true of Augustine, the moving scene in the garden would have been the climax of his spiritual history and the account of the *Confessions* would have best been brought to a close with this scene or with his baptismal peace. But, to use Augustine's own comparison, as the pilgrim of God emerged from the desert and entered into the Promised Land, a lofty vision awaited him and revealed at once the end of his journey and the peace of the plain that stretched at his feet. And Monica was again there, urging him on with maternal love and Christian piety (*Conf.*, IX, 8), opening his eyes and showing him the way.

*
* *

The place was Ostia, a short time after his baptism. Italy, the providential scene of Augustine's action and even more of his passion, had witnessed his conversion. But now Africa seemed to be claiming him for the divine work. Thus Augustine was preparing to embark with his mother and some friends when one day, while he was alone with Monica in the recess of a window, they began to talk quietly about the things of heaven. In a lengthy period that constitutes the first part of this account of this famous ecstasy, Augustine describes the setting of the scene and clearly states the general theme of the mystical conversation. The original Latin should be read if at all possible.

> As the day was drawing near on which she was to depart from this life—a day which You knew although we did not—it came about, as I believe, through Your hidden designs that she and I stood alone leaning in a certain window from which could be seen the garden within the house where we were staying. This was at Ostia on the Tiber, where away from the din of the crowd we were resting from the fatigue of our long journey in preparation for the sea voyage. And being alone together we were talking very quietly, 'and forgetting the things that were behind and looking forward to those that were to come' we

> were seeking in the presence of Truth, which You are, what the eternal life of the Saints was to be 'which eye hath not seen, nor ear heard, neither hath it entered into the heart of man to know.' But we eagerly opened the lips of our hearts to the heavenly stream of Your fountain, the fountain of Life which is with You, in order that being sprinkled from it according to our capacity, we might to some degree consider so great a subject.

This is followed by two long periods of remarkable rhythm: the first recounts in indirect discourse the conversation preceding the ecstasy; the second relates in direct discourse what followed. However, these two periods are strikingly similar in many ways and the two sections of the dialogue exhibit perfect continuity. The two texts are quite short and should be cited.

> Our conversation, (continues Augustine) led us to the conclusion that the pleasures of the bodily senses, even when seen in the brightest corporeal light, are not only unworthy of comparison with the happiness of such a life, but unworthy even to mention. And then, rising up towards 'Being itself' in a burst of love, we gradually passed beyond all corporeal things, even the very heavens from where the sun and moon and stars shine upon the earth. And we continued to mount higher, meditating, discussing, and admiring Your works within ourselves, and we came to our minds and went beyond them in order that we might arrive at that region of inexhaustible abundance where You satiate Israel forever with the food of truth. There Life is Wisdom, that Wisdom through whom all these things are made, both what has been and what shall be, and it itself is uncreated; for it *is* as it always has been and ever shall be. Or rather, to have been and to come to be

have no place in it, but only to be, since it is eternal. And while we were speaking of this Wisdom and panting after it, we touched it for an instant in a supreme leap of our hearts. And then we sighed and leaving bound to it the 'first fruits of the Spirit' we returned to the empty sound of our own tongues, where the word has a beginning and comes to an end. For what is like to your Word, Our Lord, who subsists forever in Himself without every growing old, and who makes all things new?

And so we said: 'Let us suppose that the tumult of a man's flesh were to grow silent, silent the images of earth, water, and air, silent the heavens; that his very soul were to grow silent and by not thinking of itself were to rise above itself; that all dreams and imaginary visions; that every tongue and every sign and every contingent being were to grow silent; in short, that a man were to find all things still (for one who listens to them, hears them say in unison: "We did not make ourselves, but He who made us abides forever;" that having said this, they should remain silent--since they have turned his ear to Him who made them). Let us suppose that now He alone were to speak, not by means of these creatures, but by Himself, that we might hear His word not by any tongue of flesh nor angel's voice, not by the din of thunder nor the riddle of a parable, but that we might hear Him whom we love in these creatures, Him and not them: just as we but now reached out and in a flash of the mind touched that eternal Wisdom which subsists above all things. Let us suppose that this contact were to continue, that all other visions of an inferior order were to disappear, and that this one alone were to enrapture the beholder, were to absorb and wrap him in interior joy, that his life were to be eternally just as this moment of understanding after which we sighed. . ., would this not be the realization of the words: "Enter into the joy of Thy Lord"?

> And when shall this be? Will it not be "When we shall all rise again but shall not all be changed"?
>
> Such things were we speaking, (continues Augustine in the fourth and final section of his account of the vision at Ostia,) although not in this very manner nor in these very words. But You know, O Lord, that on that day when we were speaking of these things, when this world and all its pleasures lost their appeal as we spoke, my mother said: 'My son, for my part, there is no longer anything in this life that pleases me. What have I still to do here? Why am I here? I do not know. I have at last been granted what I longed for in this world. I wished to remain alive a little longer for one thing alone: that I might see you a Catholic Christian before I died. God has granted me this grace in abundance; for I already see you his servant, despising earthly happiness. What then am I doing here?"

Monica was not to remain much longer on the earth she wished to leave. Five or six days later, she took to bed with a fever. On the ninth day of her illness, after asking prayers for her deliverance, she gave up her soul to God. She was in her fifty-sixth year; Augustine in his thirty-third.

With the death of Monica and the vision at Ostia which was a prelude to it, the story of Augustine's conversion, of his "exodus from Egypt," as he called it in biblical terms, comes to an end. Not without some justification have certain critics wished to consider the tenth book of the *Confessions* a later addition, an appendix of sorts which does not form an integral part of the work; for in this book Augustine does indeed describe his state of soul at the very time he was writing his autobiography. Also, the last three books, although they make very interesting reading for anyone capable of understanding them and are certainly not superfluous, are still not strictly necessary. The tragic and eventful journey of the convert was clearly brought to an end with the death of Monica. Another journey began. Augustine was no longer moving from error to truth or from sin to grace; he was striving to penetrate more intimately a truth already known, to nurture a spiritual seed already planted in his soul. To speak as Augustine, he was no longer engaged in a long and laborious Exodus; he was entering into the Blessed Land where milk and honey flow in abundance. He was no longer struggling to acquire a rich inheritance, the faith of his mother and of the Church, he was involved in the unending inventory of this legacy which was at once human and divine.

Without the vision at Ostia, Augustine would have been deprived of part of his sacred patrimony. Without this experience, his conversion would have been largely a matter of radical detachment; with it, his conversion involved overwhelming attachment. During this experience God certainly "freed" Augustine but, most importantly, he "laid hold of him." When paralleled with Newman's conversion, Augustine's seems richer in virtualities. In the *Essay on Development*, published the year after his abjuration, Newman expresses explicitly, if not definitively, his most important ideas, those which are strictly speaking his own and which were to bring him great renown. Shortly after his own conversion, Augustine had still written only the *Dialogues* of Cassiciacum, works so faintly characteristic of his Christian teaching that some critics have erroneously wished to place them in opposition to the writings of the second period of his life. Not until quite some time after baptism would he write such religious masterpieces as the *De trinitate* and the *De civitate Dei*. After 1844, Newman went into hiding, so that twenty years later when he published his *Apologia pro vita sua*, his own *Confessions*,

Manning would say of the book: "It is a voice from beyond the grave." On the contrary, after 386, Augustine came out of the shadows. He rapidly became one of the most influential pastors of the African Church and, indeed, of the universal Church. As the years went by, his authority grew only stronger and suffered no decline. Furthermore, the conversion of Newman was first and foremost intellectual, whereas Augustine's was principally moral. In becoming a member of the Catholic Church, the Oxford theologian experienced no positive enrichment, no unusual religious experience, he simply attained great peace in the possession of truth. His mysticism--if there is a mysticism--is calm and solitary. On the other hand, both in the garden and later at Ostia, the Milanese rhetorician was stirred to the very depths of his soul. Discovery followed discovery and his mysticism--for he does have a mysticism--is contagious and passionate. Nevertheless, Newman and Augustine do resemble one another, inasmuch as their written works are simply the translation of a vital experience and in so far as the life of each was totally present in the moment of conversion. But for Newman, conversion was principally, though not exclusively, the journey's end, whereas for Augustine, baptism, together with his consciousness in the vision at Ostia of all that baptism washes away, gives, and promises, was the journey's end and more, it was the beginning of another journey.

CHAPTER TWO

The Sources

Dicebamus ergo: "si cui
sileat tumultus carnis. . ."
(*Conf.*, IX, 25)

The primary importance of the vision at Ostia in the *Confessions*, of the *Confessions* in the corpus of Augustine's writings, and of his works in the development of Church doctrine, oblige us to make an attentive and close study of this experience and of the pages in which it is described. But before we attempt to discover its psychological organization, to determine its doctrinal significance, and to trace its influence throughout the works of the bishop and Western thought, it would be well to study this experience from the philological point of view. Now the philologist is a type of scientist, he operates on texts, and we shall witness a cold dissection of this account from the *Confessions* to uncover its literary sources. The existence of these sources is no figment of the imagination and their discovery requires no sleight of hand. All we have to do is quietly study the general lay of the land and determine the promising areas; we may then dig with firm determination to the necessary depths.

Some time has elapsed since attention was last directed to the connection between the vision at Ostia and certain lines of the *Enneads* of Plotinus. But what passages in Augustine have not been reputed to have Neoplatonic ancestry? Moreover, before we can determine which treatises of the Egyptian philosopher exerted an influence upon the *Confessions*, and in particular upon the ecstasy in Book IX, we must have more numerous bits of evidence than are generally advanced and a more perfect convergence of this evidence.

If a technical study of the literary aspects of this passage has not hitherto been made, it is because the proper instruments have not been available. We know, of course, that certain "books of the Platonists" did exert an influence upon Augustine, but the assertion has been made that this influence is more clearly discernible in the *Dialogues* than in the *Confessions*. Critics have been particularly hesitant to identify these Platonic philosophers. Does this vague expression designate Plato himself or Plotinus, as one widespread opinion would have it, or simply his disciple Porphyry? As a result of poor orientation, research has yielded only uncertain, vague, and questionable results: for want of direction, scholarship has been haphazard. Yet a return to the clearest documents of tradition and to the explicit testimony of Augustine, plus a bit of luck, will make it possible to clarify this confused and confusing situation.

In his treatise *On the Happy Life*, which we are certain was written at Cassiciacum a few months after his conversion, Augustine tells us that at least the apparent origin of this work is to be found in "a very small number of the books of Plotinus." This, then, identifies the "works of the Platonists" mentioned in the *Confessions* and saves us the trouble of delaying over long lists of treatises which Augustine might have read at Milan. It is much more important to know what he actually did read at that time and this is possible. Among these *paucissimi libri* figures most probably the treatise *On the Three Principal Hypostases* (*Enn.*, V, 1) and certainly the treatise *On the Beautiful* (*Enn.*, I, 6).[1] The *De civitate Dei* contains two literal quotations from the treatise *On the Beau-*

tiful, and Augustine again cites or paraphrases the final selection of this work twice in the *Confessions:* first in Book VII which begins with a sentence formally acknowledging the debt; then in Book VIII in the account of the scene in the garden. Thus, the treatise *On the Beautiful* was certainly one of the works which he read at Milan. Not surprisingly he devoured it eagerly; in the heat of enthusiasm he himself had written an essay on the same subject some years before. Thus, Plotinus was able to work his way into the young rhetorician's mind and even to lead him to a purely spiritual conception of beauty and divinity.

*

* *

Thanks to these precise references, we have discovered the exact passages in the *Enneads* which inspired certain sections of Augustine's works, and can now proceed confidently to study his process of adaptation and the character of his originality. Accordingly, our study of sources will not be made with an eye to the hypothetical reconstruction of a lost work, but rather to come to a better understanding of an extant work through comparison and contrast. Therefore, the *Enneads* will be of great value in our study of the *Confessions* and of the *City of God*; for they are certainly the only Greek philosophical works read by Augustine that have come down to us in their entirety. In a way, we are present at the birth of these works of Augustine and can determine both the extent of what is borrowed and of what must be attributed to the author's originality. In this respect, the two "Plotinian" passages of the *Confessions* are remarkable for their close fidelity, a fidelity in intellectual structure and general progression of ideas, to certain sections of the *Enneads*. Yet this fidelity is combined with great liberty and perfect freedom in detail and literary presentation, and with an obvious difference of opinion about certain fundamental conceptions of life. In brief, to use a convenient distinction, if these passages exhibit the same vocabulary and mentality as certain sections of the *Enneads*--and the vocabulary is not always the same--the spirit is quite different.

Together with the treatise *On the Beautiful*, Augustine also probably read the treatise *On the Three Principal Hypostases*. Here he certainly came upon the elements of his parallel between the Plotinian *Logos* and the *Word* of the Johannine Prologue, that famous parallel which begins the final and decisive phase of his account of his own conversion.

As has been shown elsewhere, the fact that Augustine read these two treatises is sufficient to account for the role played by the *Enneads* in his religious experiences at Milan and to give a satisfactory explanation of the entire Plotinian substratum of Books VII and VIII of the *Confessions*. But even more important is the fact that the vision at Ostia in Book IX leads us back again to the same two treatises, and to the second especially.

In the introduction to this treatise, the first section of the fifth *Ennead*, Plotinus states the principle that the soul should ascend to the supreme being by degrees. He then makes an application of this principle and continues:

> Let the soul examine the great universal soul, which is distinct from it but by no means a lowly soul, to see if by means of its quiet attitude it has freed itself from those things which deceive and allure others and has become worthy to look upon it. Let us suppose that the same quiet exists within the body which envelops it and that its tumult is stilled and that quiet even pervades all that lies about it: the earth,

> the sea, the air, and the very heavens which are superior to the other elements.
>
> *Enn.* V, 1, 2.

To describe this state, the Greek of the *Enneads* uses but a single word: "quiet." The Latin of the *Confessions* likewise artfully employs a single word which serves as a refrain. The word *sileant*. . .*sileant*. . .*sileant*. . .punctuates Augustine's strophes, as ησυχω. . .ησυχον. . .ησυχος. . .the phrases of Plotinus.

In addition to the "four elements," earth, water, air, and fire, the fire which according to the physics of Aristotle has its natural place in the celestial sphere, these texts also mention what Plotinus calls "the tumult of the body" or, as Augustine expresses it in more colorful terms, "the tumult of the flesh." Moreover, this "tumult of the flesh" has upset the balance of the soul. There is, therefore, a rigidly ascending gradation: man's body, the elements which surround it, then the soul with all its powers. Among these, says Augustine, are the powers of dreaming and of imaginary visions which we must rise above or, as Plotinus had said in similar though not identical terms, deceptive illusions and magical allurements from which we must free ourselves.

Augustine, a writer of consumate art and a rhetorician to his fingertips, reorganized in a skillful and majestic period the ideas and expressions which the less developed text of Plotinus offered him. Rather than repeat the word ησυχος "quiet," three times, as Plotinus had done, he has repeated it five or six times and by a stroke of genius made it correspond to the word "silence," which describes the attention of the listener. This insight was perhaps also suggested by his reading of the conclusion of the same treatise of the *Enneads:*

> If we are to perceive these objects which are present, we must turn our perceptive faculty within ourselves and fix our attention there. Just as the man who is anxious to hear a desired voice turns away from other sounds and gives ear to the one he considers best when this sound comes to him, so here we must let all sensible noises go by, except those which are necessary, and must preserve the perceptive power of the soul intact and be prepared to hear the voices from above.
>
> *Enn.*, V, 1, 12

For Augustine, this voice from above is the eternal divine word, the Word. He also enumerates the "other sounds" which must be avoided: a tongue of flesh, the voice of an angel, the din of thunder, the riddle of a parable. These things say to the heart that listens to them: "He who made us abides forever." This is a translation into biblical language and imagery of a thought that occurs in the treatise *On the Hypostases* and is expressed in a more philosophical manner in the treatise *On the Beautiful*: "In this ascent," says Plotinus, "we must put aside all that is foreign to God, that we may see him by ourselves in his solitude, in his simplicity and purity, the being upon whom all things depend, towards whom all look, through whom all exist, live and think; for he is the cause of life, intelligence and being. If we should see this being, what love and desire would we not experience in our longing to be united to him!" Remember these words, we shall come upon traces of them in Augustine's writings. Plotinus continues:

> What amazement will accompany this delight! For he who has not even seen him is able to tend towards him as towards a good; but he who has seen him becomes enamored of his beauty, becomes filled with awe and delight, lapses into a state of blissful astonishment, he loves with a

> true love, with ardent desire, he mocks other loves and scorns all that once seemed beautiful. What are we to believe they experience who see beauty in all its purity, unburdened with flesh and matter, *transcending* heaven and earth in utter purity? All other beauties are participated, composite, secondary, and come from this beauty. Thus if we should behold that being who communicates beauty to all things, who gives beauty *while remaining within itself* and who receives nothing, *if we should rest in contemplation* while possessing it, what beauty would we still lack? For this, the true and primal beauty, makes its lovers beautiful and worthy of being loved.
>
> *Enn.*, I, 6, 7.

These lines, which have already been shown to have influenced the formulation of the ecstasy at Milan, were still present in the neophyte's thought at Ostia, when he and Monica, discussed the happiness of heaven. Alluding to a mystical experience, as Plotinus had done, Augustine says, "we now reached out and in a flash of the mind"--another Plotinian expression--"touched that eternal Wisdom which *subsists above all things*. Let us suppose that this contact were to *continue*, that all other visions of an inferior order were to vanish and that this one alone were to enrapture the beholder"--also an echo of Plotinus--"were to absorb and wrap him in interior joy, that life were to be eternally just as this moment of understanding after which we sighed. . ." and he concludes the sentence with some quotations from scripture. The immutability of God, the transcendence and plenitude of divine Beauty which is the source of all beauty, the contact which one would wish to be prolonged, rapture, pleasure, and awe in this contact, all of these themes which are found in the *Confessions* can be traced to the same passages from the same two small treatises of the *Enneads*.

*

* *

We can likewise trace these two sources, treatises I, 6 and V, 1 of Plotinus, a majority of the ideas contained in the period written in indirect discourse which precedes the one just analyzed.

"After we have admired the sensible world," remarks Plotinus, "for its grandeur, its beauty and the order of its eternal movement, the gods who are in it, gods both visible and invisible"--Augustine here particularizes and speaks of the "sun, moon, and stars"--"let us ascend to the archetype and to an archetype that is more *true*, let us survey all intelligible creatures which have their interior self-knowledge and life in this eternal archetype; let us survey the pure Intelligence who presides over them, and the prodigious *Wisdom* and *Life*, the genuine life under the reign of Kronos, the God who is *satiety* and intelligence." Perhaps Augustine had this sentence in mind when he wrote: "And we came to our own minds (*mentes* for νοητα) and went beyond them in order that we might arrive at that region of inexhaustible abundance where You *satiate* Israel forever with the food of truth. There *Life is Wisdom* . . ."

Not only do the same ideas, the same associations of ideas and, indeed, the same images occur, but they are organized in the same fashion. Augustine continues: "and there *Life is Wisdom,* that Wisdom through which all these things are made, both what has been and what shall be, and it itself is uncreated; for it *is* as it always has been and ever shall be. Or rather, to have been and to come to be have no place in it, but only to be, since it is eternal." Plotinus continues:

> The Intelligence is all things; it possesses everything immutably within

> itself and identified with itself, it simply *is*, and the word *is* applies to it forever; not for an instant is it about to be; for even at this instant it *is*: nor has it been; for in this region nothing passes away, here all beings are eternally present.

Plotinus had also said that our minds are quite unlike this Intelligence, that time, a weak imitation of eternity, constrains them to turn from one thing to consider another, that one image follows another, and that they never grasp more than a segment of reality. Augustine's period also closes with this same thought: "And we returned to the empty sound of our own tongues, where the word has a beginning and comes to an end. For what is like to your Word, Our Lord, who subsists forever in himself without ever growing old and makes all things new?"

Thus the two complementary sections of the conversation between Monica and Augustine at Ostia exhibit many close affinities with two of the most famous treatises of Plotinus. And famous they are indeed. Modern scholars have been attracted to the treatise *On the Beautiful*, have commented upon it, and have translated it with great care.[1] The essay *On the Three Hypostases*, which has also drawn their attention, perhaps exerted a greater influence upon the ancients and, in particular, upon the Fathers of the Church and the ecclesiastical writers, Eusebius, Basil, Cyril of Alexandria, and Theodoret.[2]

If we were forced to confine ourselves to comparative analysis of the passages in question, we could strictly speaking deny that these two treatises were really the literary sources of the vision at Ostia. We could dispute the similarity between each of Augustine's translations or borrowings and its presumed original and, consequently, the dependence of the *Confessions* upon the *Enneads*. But we are not so constrained and thus this dependence can be established in other ways. Augustine himself has told us *both* that he read a few works of Plotinus *and* that he made use of them in at least one of his ecstasies, the one which, for the sake of brevity, may be called contemplation at Milan.

Furthermore, we know with certainty the title of one of these works, the *De pulchro*, and even without taking into account the vision at Ostia there is every indication that the treatise *On the Three Hypostases* also numbered among them and was employed, whether closely or freely, in the composition of the *Confessions*. It should be noted, however, that a whole section of this last treatise passed almost verbatim into the account of the vision at Ostia and that the very ideas that form the fabric of this account are also expressed in the treatise of Plotinus.

The *De civitate Dei* mentions the full title of Plotinus' work, *On the Three Hypostases*, and it is the only treatise to receive this honor (*Civ.* X, xxiii). This same work also contains an exact quotation of a Plotinian phrase which the bishop applied to "eternal life" just as he does in the vision at Ostia. Now, this phrase is taken from *De pulchro* which, as we have seen, served as an outline for the contemplation at Milan. Thus the more we study these texts, the more precise and numerous the indications become.

Comparing the mystical description of Book VII--which was explicitly presented as Neoplatonic and implicitly as Plotinian--and that of Book IX of the *Confessions* with the treatises of the *Enneads* which served as their models, we come to realize that these same two treatises were not only their models, but that Augustine made use of them in the same way, accurately and yet with a certain amount of freedom.

Because the section of the vision at Ostia written in direct discourse begins with a phrase recalling a phrase of the *De pulchro* and ends with a phrase which is an obvious reminiscence of the treatise *On the Three Hypostases* and because this same reminiscence can also be found with an exact reference in the *City of God,* we can rest assured that we have rediscovered at least the literary sources of the vision at Ostia in these two studies by Plotinus. This philological fact poses a psychological problem.

NOTES

1. At the beginning of the nineteenth century, the foremost editor of Plotinus, F. Creuzer, published a separate edition of Περι του καλου with commentary. At the beginning of the twentieth century, the greatest translator of the *Enneads,* Stephen MacKenna, foreshadowed his masterpiece with a small volume, *Plotinus, On the Beautiful.*

2. See Paul Henry, *Les Etats du texte de Plotin* (Paris, 1938), pp. 125-140; pp. 159-196.

CHAPTER THREE

Thought

Qui bibit ex aqua hac
sitiet iterum.
(*John*, 4, 13)

The psychological significance of the vision at Ostia is profound and manifold. We can easily distinguish three strong pressures. In the teaching of the *Enneads*, we find the dynamism of philosophy and of the eternal and absolute demands of thought; in the influence of scripture, the dynamism of the faith of the Church together with the sense of decisive events, of history, and of tradition; in the presence of a mother beside her son, the concrete dynamism of Christian life, alive and superbly lived in an extraordinary soul.

These forces had been exerting a continual influence upon one another long before they affected Augustine. Christian life draws its nourishment from the scriptures, yet it is quite possible that the scriptures owe something to Greek philosophy. On the other hand, the *Enneads* were written in Rome, the center of Christianity, breathing its atmosphere and retaining something of its indescribable mystic fragrance. Neither simple nor clearly defined, these forces are nevertheless distinct. We can observe each of them at work, can study their fusion and opposition, can follow their constant growth in the convert's soul, and can analyze the ultimate realization of their potentialities.

A study of the final product of these forces will give us

a better understanding of the internal law which governs them. If we see what Augustine became, we will be able to observe more effectively what he was in the process of becoming. For in the innermost depths of the soul lies an internal finality independent of the material and external world. During its period of growth, the soul is obedient to certain laws which appear least obscurely, perhaps, in its final stage of development.

This does not mean that these different elements are united in the vision at Ostia by simple addition, that these packets of energy are merely juxtaposed. A synthesis is never reducible to the algebraic sum of its parts. Life itself is quite different from and superior to an immense chemical reaction.

The vision at Ostia assumes a meaning and orientation which cannot be reduced to either the meaning or orientation of any of its component parts. The resultant force is new, original, and in a certain sense unique.

Augustine's personality and the depth of his specifically religious aspirations have singled him out as one of the most perfect prototypes of the convert and, more generally, of the Christian. Although his experiences are profoundly personal, they are nevertheless so rich and so full that souls of every age and every land have been able to recognize in his descriptions their own finest and most beautiful experiences. The *Confessions*, a history of a soul's journey toward God, clearly has the same psychological significance and the same doctrinal range as the *City of God*, an epic of the entire human race on its way towards its Creator.

*

*   *

Plotinian elements played a large part in the vision at Ostia. Some critics would be willing to say that they are too much in evidence. As a matter of fact, the study of literary sources has shown us how deeply Augustine absorbed not only a few of Plotinus' ideas but even his cast of mind. He not merely clothed his thoughts in the same words and images; he adopted the same progression of ideas.

Having just read the *Enneads*, it was only natural that Augustine should have turned to their vocabulary and should have been influenced by their style in his expression of the thoughts and inspirations which they aroused in him. We should expect such a reaction and should not be at all surprised that the contemplation at Milan, which describes the impression made upon Augustine's soul by his reading of the "Platonists," is patterned after a Plotinian model and traces the philosophical lines of the treatise *On the Beautiful*. The fact that Augustine did not disguise his true feelings, did not try to minimize the importance of his pagan masters, but rather explicitly acknowledged them, is proof of the clarity of his judgment and sincerity of his statements.

However, Augustine's reading of the *Enneads* was followed by meditation on the scriptures. St. Paul, the Prophets, and the Psalmists took the place of Plotinus. Dialectics made room for prayer. In the solitude of Cassiciacum, the convert prepared to "give his name" to the Church. Consequently, we should expect that the feelings, doctrinal preoccupations, and ideas of the newly-baptized will no longer be exactly the same as those of the catechumen, and that the vision at Ostia will not be a mere reduplication of the meditation at Milan. In point of fact, Augustine does not present the vision at Ostia as an ecstasy which has its origin in his philosophical reading, but rather as a supernatural anticipation of "eternal life" as it is revealed to the Christian soul of Monica through the scriptures and tradition of the Church. Just as St. Bernard and then Beatrice come to replace Virgil at Dante's side in the *Divine Comedy*, so here, Augustine no longer takes a "Neoplatonist swollen with monstrous pride" as guide in his spiritual journey, but rather a servant of God who is pious and good, his gentle mother Monica.

Yet this mystical ascent follows the same pattern as the *Enneads*. There is no need to delay on this point. Contempt, or rather total forgetfulness of the sensible world, the impulse toward the world of spirit, repose in the world of ideas where all is truth, eternity, and satiety, the very brevity of this moment of union, and finally the disenchanted return to the inferior realm of the senses and of human speech, all of these are key notions, ideas, and attitudes which Plotinus would not have disavowed. Then in the dialogue in direct discourse, which may well be accurately reported, we find those striking expressions which describe the quiet of all things and of the soul, complete renunciation, the joy, the rapture that secures contact with the Absolute, all of these expressions are clearly taken directly from the *Enneads*. The use of that literary technique by which things speak to the soul also recalls the two great personifications found in the *Enneads:* one "concerning time" (*Enn.*, III, 7, 11); the other "concerning nature" (*Enn.*, III, 8, 4). In both instances, the creature is personified in Augustine. In short, the most striking passages in the treatises *On the Beautiful* and *On the Hypostases*, those which once read or heard imprint themselves forever upon the memory, those which Augustine certainly recalled more slowly as the years went by, all of these passages might be said to shine through the narrative of the *Confessions*. And yet Augustine does not employ any anonymous quotations throughout this section, he attributes the origin of the thoughts and words which Monica and he then exchanged entirely to his mother and himself. This silence is revealing. In the lucid mind of Augustine, the vision at Ostia typifies specifically religious and Christian experience. An edition of the *Confessions* containing a critical apparatus indicating allusions to the scriptures will reveal the surprising abundance of scriptural references. In these two pages alone there are nearly a dozen.

Although, as we shall see, Augustine had translated some of his philosophical concepts into biblical language by the time he began to write his autobiography, nevertheless, the conversation with his mother in the spring of 387 is unquestionably Plotinian in mentality. Because we possess the complete *Enneads* and have been able to make a close study of their structure, we can argue that all of these notions, which can be found today in the legacies of Judaism or Christianity, had their origin in the two treatises which overwhelmed Augustine a few months before his conversion. Some of his most characteristic ideas are Plotinian, witness the dialectic of ascent so obvious here and elsewhere throughout the *Confessions* that it reveals the influence of the *Enneads*, and the mystical renunciation marked by a strongly negative stress which can be found in neither the Gospels, nor St. Paul, nor St. John. Indeed the thread of unity that binds these ideas together and the inspiration that permeates them are equally Plotinian.

The account of this event, composed some ten or eleven years after it actually occurred, is unquestionably as Neoplatonic as the experience itself. If Augustine did not designate it as such, he did nothing to disguise its character. He could so easily have suppressed every trace of the *Enneads* from his ecstasy. After much difficulty in searching out the sources of numerous passages of his works, some critics maintain that he did indeed suppress the Plotinian elements, and quite effectively. Such men lack insight. They point out a few, short, scattered reminiscences of the *Enneads*, treat them as "stray passages" and, for the most part, agree upon the non-Plotinian character of the *Confessions*. They maintain that Augustine presented himself too clearly as a disciple of Christ and that such a disposition is incompatible with a follower of Plotinus.

Disagreement among critics has centered on the convert's early works. But they have not approached their task prepared to recognize the Plotinian qualities of the *Confessions*. Some have been principally concerned with minimizing the role of the Platonists in Augustine's conversion and with diminishing their importance in the formation of his philosophy and theology. Others have been content to place the early *Dialogues*, which they maintain are the work of a philosopher, in marked contrast to the *Confessions*, which they denounce as an apologetic work and therefore one of questionable value. They have considered his early *Dialogues* sincere, trustworthy, and strictly Plotinian in inspiration; looking upon the *Confessions* as a romantic autobiography written for edification, they have gradually shut their eyes to the Plotinian character of certain passages. Now, at least, we must recognize the fact that the *Confessions* are no less Plotinian than the *Dialogues*.

*

* *

At first glance, a Christian might think it unfortunate that a passage as beautiful as the account of the vision at Ostia was directly inspired by the *Enneads*. For want of a sufficiently broad and deep notion of religion, he might regret that an experience, which he justly considers a superior and unique manifestation of the life which flows within the large body of which he is a member, does not appear to be utterly and entirely Christian and transcendent.

Augustine would surely not have shared such regrets. He who affirmed that the Platonists had only to change "some of their expressions and ideas" in order to become Christian, would have been happy to extol the beauty, harmony, and loftiness of human reason, and of its metaphysical constructions. He would willingly have acknowledged all that he owed to Plotinus in his account of the vision at Ostia and, indeed, in the very origin of this vision. He would have applied to himself, as he does in analogous circumstances, the symbolic and prophetic episode of Exodus. Had God not ordered the Israelites to carry away with them the "spoils of Egypt"? Augustine was too keenly aware of the singular originality of Christian doctrine to fear that it might appear inferior beside any philosophical system, no matter how lofty it might be. He was too well aware of the tremendous scandal the revelation of an Incarnate God would be for "the Gentiles" and the Platonists to fear that he would be accused of plagiarism on this essential point. In the natural harmony between the spiritualistic system of Plotinus and the Johannine doctrine on the divinity of the Word, between the metaphysical attraction of the many towards the One and the aspiration of the Christian soul for the face-to-face vision of God, he had glimpsed a proof and, as it were, a sensible sign of the universality and native catholicity of Christianity, of its power and obligation to adapt.

If the message of the Church is transcendent, the words she employs to transmit it are not. Augustine himself recalled the example of St. Paul on the Areopagus preaching the Unknown God, to whom the Athenians had erected an altar, and quoting to them the words of one of their own poets concerning the supernatural sonship of man. Augustine explicitly connected this incident with his own relationship to pagan philosophy. When he adopts Platonism as a mode of expression and even, as we shall see, when he looks upon it with respect and sympathy as a witness of the divinity of the Word, he remains faithful of the tradition of the Church which in the thirteenth century led St. Thomas to rethink its doctrine in peripatetic terms, and which in the twentieth century imposes an obligation upon the Catholic theologian to make this teaching accessible to modern thought and thus to elevate to it, as in time gone by, the intelligentsia as well as the ordinary run of men.

It is hard to believe that Neoplatonism would have been merely a means of expression for the visionary at Ostia, a superficial covering which he could have removed without impoverishing himself, as one throws off old clothes to put on new ones, or even like vestments which one puts on for a sacred ceremony and afterwards lays aside while remaining unchanged.

Augustine never denied the firm convictions he owed to the Platonists any more than he blindly accepted their conception of life. Later in his *Retractationes* he would reproach himself for having been excessive in his praise of "these unbelieving men," but this was only after he had so assimilated their teachings that he could no longer distinguish them from his own. It was at an age when he was more shocked by error than fascinated by truth, especially those natural truths once learned from the Platonists and long since transcended. Modern interpreters are occasionally over-zealous and do Augustine an injustice when they maintain that Neoplatonism slowly disintegrated in his mind and by a sort of spontaneous generation or miracle made way for some divinely inspired Christian philosophy. This is simply not the case. Platonism, penetrating ever more deeply into Augustine's soul, finally took solid root, became integrated with the *philosophia perennis*, and entered once and for all into the patrimony of human thought. If the teachings of the Gospels were greatly vitalized by the *Enneads*, upon which Augustine had grafted them, in return, this last branch of Greek philosophy owes to the staunch tree of Christianity its salvation, if not from oblivion, at least from death. For it was in a perilous situation and even in Augustine's time had ceased to be cultivated.

CHAPTER FOUR

Revelation

> Qui autem biberit ex aqua quam ego dabo ei, non sitiet in aeternum.
> (*John*, 4, 14)

Even in the vision at Ostia the fusion of Neoplatonism and Christianity is very intimate and appears more essential and vital in passages where we would have expected such an integration to have taken place more slowly or less completely. At least some of the biblical texts, which we would have thought had a fixed meaning, become malleable in the hands of Augustine and are used to express ideas other than those intended by the sacred author.

Before we go any further, however, we must determine the authenticity of these scriptural expressions. There are serious reasons to doubt that all of them were used in the actual dialogue between mother and son. When Augustine writes, "such things were we speaking, although not in this very manner nor in these very words," he is putting us on our guard against excessively naive confidence. Some will object to the application of this caution to the biblical language of the vision at Ostia, rather than to its Plotinian structure. However, we have already seen that this structure underlies the entire account. In Book VII, where Augustine is actually imitating the *Enneads* quite closely and calls our attention to that fact, he prefaces his exposition with the very same warning. Now the present passage exhibits the same fidelity to sources and the sources are still the same. Therefore, we can rest assured that the framework of the vision at Ostia is just as Plotinian as the framework of the contemplation at Milan. But in the vision at Ostia, we come upon a new phenomenon, new at least in the degree to which it is present.

To be sure, scriptural allusions abound throughout the *Confessions*. Augustine had been nourished by the scriptures and it is only natural that he should have borrowed their language. Thus we should not be surprised if he uses biblical terms to express ideas, experiences, and even an entire conversation which were originally a shade more secular and intellectual, less emotional and religious. In the considerations which follow the ecstasy at Milan in chapter x and xii of Book VII and which develop a theory of evil in close dependence upon the theory expressed in the *Enneads*, the vocabulary and mentality remain totally philosophical. But in the vision at Ostia, if the mentality is still Plotinian, the language that expresses it is frequently scriptural.

A few examples will allow us to appreciate Augustine's style and the appropriate astonishment it provokes. In the personification of creatures, which is most probably Plotinian, the *non ipsa nos fecimus* of the Psalms appears simply to express the total dependence of creatures upon the Absolute, much as Plotinus expresses it in the passage which is here Augustine's source of inspiration. Also, the "first fruits of the Spirit" is clearly a translation into Pauline terms of what Augustine had read in the *Enneads*. "Such is the soul," the same passage continues, "which is precious and divine: with the help of such an instrument seek God in confidence and ascend to him. . .Know, then, *that the most divine part of this divine soul is the one closest to the Superior Being, after whom and from whom the soul proceeds* (*Enn.*, V, i, 3). This interpretation is confirmed by the very fact that in St.

Paul *primitias spiritus* signifies something entirely different from the highest part of the soul, the sense in which Augustine employs it. Consequently, it is also clear in this context that an expression as decidedly biblical as "in that region of inexhaustible abundance where You satiate Israel forever with the food of truth" most probably conveys an idea which Plotinus expressed in the form of a mythological allegory (the Greek word for abundance or satiety is "koros") of the god "Kronos," the personification of eternity, life, intelligence, and wisdom.

Thus a rapid study of the biblical quotations scattered throughout the account of the vision at Ostia leads to what seem to be rather startling conclusions; actually they are quite natural and should have been expected. The Plotinian images throughout this passage are by no means pure symbols of religious thought, in fact the scriptures occasionally clothe Plotinian concepts in their own language.

However, this does not mean that the Bible had no influence upon the core of the experience and the tone of the dialogue, that the scriptural language used throughout the narrative is no more a veneer. The very opposite is true. Obviously the scriptures, and especially the Epistles of St. Paul, were as important a factor in the conversion of Augustine as the *Enneads*. And so, not surprisingly, the sources of Christian revelation continued to act upon him in the vision at Ostia. We may even suppose that their influence increased as time went on. For when Augustine first came in contact with Plotinus, his knowledge of the scriptures was inadequate, but he began to study them at once and rapidly became an outstanding exegete.

Notice that the account of Augustine's conversation with Monica begins with a famous quotation from the First Epistle to the Corinthians and is brought to a close with another quotation from the same Epistle. This latter quotation, which concludes the section of the conversation written in direct discourse, seems to be quite authentic and actually to have been spoken at Ostia, while in all probability the former should be ascribed to the narrator. The second is attributable to Monica, who had meditated upon the scriptures, or to the newly-baptized; the first to the bishop who was writing the *Confessions*.

It would seem that three words found at the *climax* of a period in the first part of the narrative are no less historical. "And then," says Augustine, "rising up *towards Being itself* in a burst of love, we gradually passed beyond all corporeal things." This powerful expression, *in id ipsum*, is taken from the Fourth Psalm. Earlier in the *Confessions*, Augustine recounts how at Cassiciacum he had "cried aloud to God while reading the Psalms of David, those canticles of faith, those songs of devotion so suited to humble the spirit or pride. . .How they inflamed me with love for You, and I was stirred with desire to shout them aloud to the whole world that the pride of mankind might be brought low" (*Conf.*, IX, iv). It is remarkable, incidentally, that traditional criticism has been able to neglect such texts and sanction the legend of an Augustine at Cassiciacum, as yet unconverted, scarcely even Christian at heart, and occupied exclusively with philosophy.

On this same point, it is important to note that Augustine made the Fourth Psalm the special object of his meditation during this time. "And I wished," he says in speaking of the Manichaeans whom he had just abandoned, "that they had been somewhere near me at that time and I unaware of it, in order that they might have looked upon my face and listened to my words while during that time of leisure I read the Fourth

Psalm. . .I shuddered with fear and at the same time I became inflamed with exultant hope in your mercy, Oh Father! And all of this was expressed in my eyes and voice. . . ." He runs through the verses of the Psalm in this fashion and notes down the thoughts and feelings they aroused in him. This burning exegesis ends with the words:

> The next verse brought a *deep cry from my heart:* Oh, 'in your peace!' Oh, *'in your very Being!'* But what did he say? 'I will sleep. I will take my rest.' For who will dare to resist us when what has been written has come to pass: Death is swallowed up in victory. You are *Being itself* to a supreme degree, You who are changeless. In You is that rest which is oblivious to all troubles. For there is no one besides You. Nor am I to go in quest of other things which are not You, O Lord; 'You alone have strengthened me in hope.' These things I read and I burned. . . ."

This flame will not be soon extinguished, Fanned by Monica's breath, it will burn with a new brilliance and will radiate its warmth throughout Augustine's soul in the vision at Ostia. There is no need to stress the similarity of ideas expressed in the account of the vision and in the first meditation on the Fourth Psalm. Both treat of repose in God, of detachment from all creatures, and of the desire for eternal life. The cry uttered by Augustine as he read the ninth verse, *in id ipsum*, is prolonged and echoes from the plains of Milan to the shores of the Mediterranean.

If Augustine turned to the Bible in order to express his sentiments during the vision at Ostia, it was no mere rhetorical device. Such a technique is used frequently throughout the *Confessions*, which are decidedly biblical in tone, but here it is employed because Augustine recognized Plotinian concepts in scriptural terms. In other words, we must reject the easy and deceptive pleasure of cutting the account of the vision into "successive drafts" that we might ascribe certain elements to the period of the actual event and others to the period during which the *Confessions* were written. When Augustine relates a past conversation, he does not pretend to reproduce it word for word--he had secretaries at Cassiciacum, but none at Ostia. Nevertheless, he is careful to give us its substance and general flavor. The conversation with his mother was an amalgamation of Plotinian thought and biblical expression, and is apparently the same one we can analyze in his written work. Although some of these expressions, as we have seen, have an independent value and are a re-expression of earlier specifically religious utterances, the fact that others are made to convey ideas which are entirely Neoplatonic is even more indicative of such a fusion. This fact certainly seems to weaken the interpretation of those who hold that Augustine's debt to Plotinus is superficial and can be reduced to the use of a "vocabulary." Would Augustine have embellished his narrative with imagery and phrases from the *Enneads* merely to make himself understood by his contemporaries? This would be a rather tenuous thesis to defend. The truth of the matter is not so simple. If we maintain the distinction between conception and language, then it is equally true to say that the mentality of the vision at Ostia is clearly Plotinian and that the language which Augustine borrowed to express it is Christian; for he was writing for Christians.

If the account of the ecstasy is trustworthy, this is just as it should be. If Monica spoke and if Augustine answered her, as he says he did, they would certainly have employed scriptural terms to indicate what the scriptures promised. And if Augustine expressed his experiences according to a Platonic conception, as a loving son he would certainly have made sure that his mother understood him and would have been careful to speak a language she could understand, the language of Christianity. For the presence of Monica is the third essential element of the vision at Ostia.

CHAPTER FIVE

Christian Life

> Aqua quam ego dabo
> fiet in eo fons aquae
> salientis.
> (*John*, 4, 14)

Even limited to its constitutive elements, the vision at Ostia is more than a mere summation. It shows enrichment, advance, progress; it represents synthesis and evolution, whether viewed in terms of component parts or positive new elements. On this occasion, Augustine not only made use of the treasures of past experience, but enriched his life through new experience. Yet his mother's soul was the channel through which this fresh spring water came to him. Monica is the central figure of this scene, not Augustine, and the position of the vision at Ostia in Augustine's narrative is concrete proof of this claim. It is part of Book IX, that section of the *Confessions* devoted almost entirely to descriptions of the childhood, virtues, and death of St. Monica. Thus there can be no doubt that in Augustine's eyes this account was first and foremost an episode from his mother's life.

Monica's active and principal role in the ecstasy gave it an authentically and specifically Christian character. Her presence is a fact, a simple yet significant fact which cannot be ignored. Without Monica there might have been a second contemplation at Milan, but would there have been a vision at Ostia? To a great extent, she was the one who was "forgetful of the things that were behind and looking forward to those that were to come." As we have already seen, Augustine was so incapable of forgetting the past that his thoughts drew material from it. It was Monica who wanted to know what heaven had in store for her: that eternal life of the blessed which "eye hath not seen, nor ear heard, neither hath it entered into the heart of man to know." Monica had suffered greatly in the past, but now, as she stood beside her prodigal son who had returned to God and to his mother, she experienced great happiness and joy. What did the future hold in store? Now that she had been granted what she had lived and prayed and wept for, she thought of death. Monica was probably the one who turned their conversation to this subject; she was certainly the one, Augustine tells us, who brought the dialogue to a close.

Monica seems to have had very little to say. She felt compelled to ask a question about heaven, a question filled with religious yearning. Because Augustine was more learned and was steeped in the writings of Plotinus, St. Paul, and the Psalmist, because he was inspired by his mother's reflections, because he was a poet and was conscious of the silence of surrounding nature, he perceived the gentle voices of creatures, the serene and detached joys of philosophical contemplation, and the supernatural peace of the blessed resounding within his soul and uniting into a rich symphony. The dominant note of this interior concert, the one that sustained and took possession of his soul, was the thought of heaven, for which Monica was responsible. She turned towards him with a questioning glance and he began to speak. After he had pointed out the admirable spectacle that lay before their eyes, had recalled the hot passions of his youth, which he had finally managed to subdue, and had developed the Plotinian and Pauline themes which still echoed within and haunted him, he described to her the pure raptures of the spirit. Then proceeding at a more rapid pace, he struggled to go beyond human understanding and strove to attain, through the fine point of the soul, the mysterious sanctuary where God abides. He spoke--*dicebam talia*,--while Monica remained silent, impressed. Using a language she could understand, he gave expression to sentiments which he confusedly detected in her and which she communicated to him. When he reached that summit where thought is as ineffectual as language, the text implies that he also became silent and that only a sigh--*suspiravimus*--expressed the state of a soul that thrilled under the action of God. However, this moment passed quickly. Augustine began to speak again--*remeavimus usque ad strepitum oris nostri*--and quietly remarked: "Mother, let us suppose that this contact were to continue, would this not be heaven, the joy of the Lord, what the Apostles have promised us for the day of Resurrection?" And Monica answered: "My son, for my part, there is no longer anything in this life that pleases me. What do I still have to do here? Why am I here? I do not know. I have been granted what I longed for in this world. . . . What then am I doing here?" These words betray Monica's burning desire and give the ecstasy its full meaning. Intense Christian life and a sensitive and strong taste for the divine flowed from her soul into Augustine's. This is the characteristic element and original contribution of the vision at Ostia, what distinguishes it from the meditations, prayers, and "visions," if you will, which preceded it. If Augustine had previously failed to experience some dimension of religious conversion, it was neither the rational conviction nor simple faith of the neophyte, neither the docile humility nor burning charity of the disciple of Christ, but the flowering of all of these, the peace and joy of mystical possession.

The mention of mystical experience brings up a difficulty. How could a conversation between two human beings give way to an intimate encounter between the soul and God? Clearly the Lord is not to be found in the chatter of conversation, but a soul may become inflamed through contact with another soul and the degree of influence will depend upon their intimacy with each other and of both with God. Teresa of Avila and John of the Cross, to mention but one of many illustrious examples, more than once terminated their conversations in ecstasy. At Ostia, however, Monica possessed this solitude from the very beginning and Augustine came to it mysteriously soon. They were far from the crowd--*remoti a turbis*--and alone--*soli valde dulciter*. Each in his own way was aware of this interior emptiness. They were prepared for ecstasy.

Monica was aware that Augustine would understand her perfectly, if she opened her heart to him. She poured herself out, confessing her happiness as a mother and her hopes as a Christian. In this way, she introduced into Augustine's soul sentiments and ideas which began to develop according to a singularly personal law, which unfolded according to a more skillful, more complex and harmonious pattern in which the new intuitive and vibrant element was combined with other elements, with prophecy and intellectual considerations. But the climax of this experience was not to be found in the inaudible cry of Monica or in the triumphant and melodious outpourings of Augustine, but in that unique note which was sounded within their innermost depths by a mysterious finger, upon which their souls lingered and which came after a sigh and a period of silence.

Some days later, Monica took to bed and soon after she left this world--*mundus iste*--for a better one. It was no mere accident that she did not simply lead the catechumen to the porch of the Church or even into the nave where baptisms are performed, but that she left Augustine only after she had brought him to the threshold of the sanctuary where the priesthood, the service of God and His people, awaited him--*ut servum eius videam.* Monica herself realized that she had fulfilled her earthly destiny, and that this destiny was "to bring forth Augustine according to the flesh, that he might be born into temporal life, and according to the heart, that he might be born into eternal life" (*Conf.*, IX, 17). But after the vision at Ostia, Augustine found himself enriched not only in his possession of the truths proposed by the Church, but in his intimate and personal realization of these truths. His faith was doubled by an experience. The holy of holies swung open for an instant. Monica had nothing more to do here below.

*

* *

If Monica was with Augustine at the end of his pilgrimage, it was because she had accompanied him along the way. There is no need to bring her forth from the shadows where she stands as the veiled symbol of the saintly woman. As we read the *Confessions*, it becomes evident that she exerted an incalculable, even a dominant influence, one in no way inferior to that of the philosophers and inspired authors. This is not surprising. A mother can have a profound effect upon her child's soul. And, if she is able to retain his confidence, her tenderness can exert a powerful force upon the child when he reaches manhood. A woman is instinctively careful not to put pressure upon the intelligence of one she loves; in return she appeals to the strength of feeling. She does not debate, she does not counter argument with argument, but rather with impressions, facts, and experiences. Monica, a woman and a mother, dealt with Augustine in this way. In the well-chosen and strong words of her son, she had seen to it that he drank in the sweetness of the name of Christ along with her milk (*Conf.*, III, 8). So deeply had the young mother's influence penetrated her son's heart that when the young man read Cicero's *Hortensius*, the only thing that tended to cool his enthusiasm was the fact that he did not find a mention of the sweet name of the Savior--*alte retinebat* (*Conf.*, III, 8). Christianity had been implanted within him from his earliest years--*insita*--and had worked its way into the very marrow of his bones--*medullitus* *Acad.*, II, 5).

Monica silently continued to watch over Augustine through prayers and tears. Through tears, for he was turning aside from her and from Christ to such an extent that she was horrified by his blasphemies and eventually refused for a time to live in the same house with him and to eat at the same table. During this period, Monica had a dream which allows us to determine the precise nature and extent of her influence. Augustine relates that:

> she saw herself in a dream standing on a wooden measuring rod; a radiant youth approached her cheerfully and smiled at her sadness and grief. He asked her the cause of this sorrow and of her daily tears. . . . She answered that she was lamenting the loss of my soul. He then bade her to be reassured and urged her to look carefully and to observe that where she was, I was also. She looked and declared that I was indeed beside her, standing on the same rule
>
> *Conf.*, III, 19

Monica eagerly shared this vision with her son and did not hesitate to interpret it for him as a prophetic assurance of his return to the faith. Interestingly, Augustine does not conceal the fact that he was impressed, if not by the very content of the dream, at least by his mother's confidence and serenity.

A short time later, she applied the same interpretation to the now-famous words of the bishop whom she had plagued to talk with Augustine. Accurately judging the moment inopportune, Ambrose sent her away with these words: "Go, leave me alone, as truly as you live, it is impossible that the son of these tears should perish" (*Conf.*, III, 21). She looked upon these words as a message from heaven and did not fail to mention this to Augustine.

So great was Monica's hold upon Augustine that, when he left Carthage for Italy, he feared that she might follow him and took flight by night, leaving her praying on shore near a chapel of St. Cyprian. This was not a sign of harshness, as some have thought, but the sign of a conscience sharpened by Monica's powerful maternal tenderness. However, such rebuffs never stop a mother. Augustine spent some months in Rome where he was disappointed by the morals of his students, but when he assumed a chair of rhetoric at Milan, Monica did not hesitate to join him again. She at once tried everything in her power to induce him to enter into personal and regular contact with Ambrose. She went about this task with an infinite amount of tact and discretion. She asked Augustine to go to the bishop for her to request some advice and some permissions for her practices of piety and works of mercy. When she saw his Manichaean convictions shaken, she did not display excessive joy, but received the news very calmly, even coldly, and told him that he had only reached the first milestone on the road to Catholicism. Monica never ceased to exhibit tranquil confidence in and a preoccupation with Augustine's ultimate conversion. Such sentiments surely made an impression upon the young man who no longer knew where to find truth.

During this period, mother and son became so communicative that they discussed a matter as personal as Augustine's marriage. Monica was hoping that once he had been delivered from the bonds of concubinage, he would be willing to be baptized. Therefore, she tried to find him a legitimate spouse. Augustine appears to have begun to believe in the supernatural character of the communications with which Monica was favored. He asked her to obtain through a dream some enlightenment from God about his marriage plan. The result was not satisfactory and Monica was not convinced of the divine origin of her thoughts on this subject. The projected union did not take place. When Augustine was in the garden at Milan reading the Epistle to the Romans, he turned in earnest to the faith of his early years and decided henceforth to live a life of continence. This decision once made, it is again revealing that he hastened to share his new joyous excitement with Monica. When Augustine comes to this point in his narrative, he recalls how Monica's dream, nine years earlier, had thus been realized: the son had returned to his mother and adhered to the same "rule of faith." Although it is not mentioned, they may well have recalled this earlier prediction during their conversations of this period. What is certain is that, as has happened in many a man's life, the son's respect for his mother strengthened and grew as the years passed and, after his conversion, as the months went by. Augustine's high esteem for Monica and for the extraordinary gifts which he recognized in her--intelligence, insight, almost divination--prepared for and partly explain the all-important role she was to play in the vision at Ostia.

*

*   *

Although this experience certainly contained all sorts of rich, new elements, it was still in line with past experiences.

More accurately, it was their prolongation and sequel. With this in mind, we must reread and study the famous *Dialogues* of Cassiciacum, which some critics claim are devoid of Christian significance, to understand more clearly the vision at Ostia and Monica's part in it. She intervened more than once in the discussions, discreetly, of course, but on matters of fundamental importance. Augustine's reactions on such occasions are typical.

The most conspicuous dialogue, from this point of view, is the *De beata vita* in which Augustine placed his mother among the most important interlocutors--*in primis nostra mater*. He says that he is indebted to her for "all that I am,"--*omne quod vivo* (*Beat.*, I, 6). The importance of the subject under discussion, the nature of happiness, greatly increases the value of each of Monica's contributions. As should be expected, Monica's interventions have a moral and religious quality which encroaches upon the philosophical tenor of the conversation and stands out in the dialogue. One of the first times she spoke, she spontaneously remarked that "if man is happy when he desires the good and possesses it, then if he desires evil and possesses it, he should experience only unhappiness." Augustine smilingly approved, "Mother, there you have the key to all philosophy," and he bolstered this opinion with a quotation from Cicero's *Hortensius*. Monica was greatly moved by this passage and Augustine delicately tells us that she uttered "such exclamations that we were oblivious of her sex and thought that we had some great man in our midst; I, for my part, tried to understand from what divine source her words derived" (*Beat.*, II, 10). This statement is not an hyperbole; it should be taken literally.

Two days later, on November 14, at the time of another of Monica's important contributions, Augustine gave expression to his thoughts. After a charming hesitation, Monica had suggested that they should not separate unhappiness--*miser esse*--from the lack of wisdom--*egere sapientia*--as they wished to do. She anticipated Augustine who intended to point out that this is one of the finest principles philosophers have discovered. He therefore hailed his mother's reflections as something astonishing and turned to his friends saying: "You see what a great difference there is between knowing many different doctrines and having a soul that is entirely devoted to God" (*Beat.*, IV, 27). Augustine always preserved the same respectful tone, almost a reverence, for Monica's "visionary" gifts.

Finally, the conversation was brought to a close with a remark, or rather a prayer, by Monica. When Monica heard the words of the dialogue defining happiness as "the perfect and holy knowledge of the Being who leads us to truth, puts us in possession of it, and unites us to what has been called the Supreme Measure," in other words the knowledge of God, she recalled the hymns of Ambrose, which were deeply imprinted upon her memory, and recited the beautiful supplicatory verse of the *Deus creator omnium,* "Hear, O Trinity, those who pray to Thee." Joyously she added: "This is undoubtedly the happy life, the perfect life, and we must be confident that a solid faith, lively hope, and burning charity can lead our eager steps to it" (*Beat.*, IV, 35). Thus, as far as Monica was concerned, it is the theological virtues, the fundamental virtues of Christianity, that lead man to happiness, and her very turn of phrase shows that she considered this happiness reserved for those who have already left this earth. Augustine the philosopher did not understand happiness in this sense. He thought that even here below our knowledge of God could be perfect and that happiness could be attained by human efforts. In the *Retractationes* he would reproach himself for not having said that complete happiness is reserved for the afterlife.

A short time later, as a small group of friends at

Cassiciacum was talking about the problem of Providence and evil, a discussion centering on the divinity of Christ led to a dispute between Licentius and Trygetius. Augustine was grieved and had to intervene to calm the ardor of his young disciples. Monica entered and asked what progress the discussion had made. Augustine told his secretary to note down Monica's entry and question She was startled and delightfully exclaimed: "Have your books never shown you a woman taking part in discussions such as these?" Her son then told her how much her philosophy pleased him, and also explained that the "Holy Scriptures, the subject of her ardent meditation," did not censure all philosophers, but only worldly ones. After he had explained that in a certain sense she herself was a philosopher, a friend of wisdom, he concluded with these charming words: "Since you love wisdom much more than you love me--and I know how much you love me--since your progress in wisdom has been so great that no unforeseen suffering, even death itself, can frighten you, and since this, as all admit, is the high point of philosophy, will I not willingly be your disciple, *egone me non libenter discipulum dabo*" (*Ord.*, I, 32)? He would indeed be her disciple in a most special way when less than a year later, shortly before her death, Monica would lead him to contemplate the afterlife.

At the beginning of the second Book of the *De ordine*, Augustine explains why he "decided that Monica should take part in these new dialogues, when she should have the leisure to do so." He tells us that "life-long intimacy and diligent study had revealed to me her mental acumen and her burning desire for things divine--*ingenium atque in res divinas inflammatum animum*--and because in the course of a very important discussion about happiness held on my birthday, her superb intellect made such an impression upon me that nothing seemed more suited for true philosophy" (*Ord.*, II, 1). Augustine's insistent return to his mother's intellectual and moral superiority clearly indicates the importance of her role in the *Dialogues* of Cassiciacum and guarantees the Christian character of his early *Dialogues*. Towards the end of the *De ordine* he says, "Mother, do not be frightened by this immense forest of knowledge. We will select only a few essential notions which many persons learn with difficulty, but which you will not find troublesome. For your mental powers are daily revealed to me anew and I know that your heart, which age or remarkable temperance has liberated from all vanities and has raised above the weakness of the body, has risen to great heights within itself" (*Ord.*, II, 45). And while the *De beata vita* is brought to a close with Monica's spontaneous prayer, in the *De ordine*, Augustine asks his mother to obtain through her intercession the grace that he might discover the truth and possess it; for it was through her that he had already obtained the grace to desire, to seek, and to love truth alone (*Ord.*, II, 52).

*

* *

As we reread the *Dialogues* of Cassiciacum with attention on Monica, the vision at Ostia becomes more intelligible. For some years, mother and son had been accustomed to intimate discussions on lofty subjects. Monica simply expressed her thoughts and Augustine took them up, developed them, and showed that they were in accord with the dicta of philosophers. Prayer was often mixed with philosophical reflection, the Holy Scriptures and religious hymns were often cited along with quotations from the great classics of human thought. Therefore, once we realize Monica's place in the *Dialogues* of Cassiciacum, we no longer have any reason to doubt that she played an essential role in the vision at Ostia.

Religion was clearly never absent at Cassiciacum, and yet Monica was really the only one who had been acquainted for any length of time with Christian practices and dogmas, with everything Augustine included under the heading of "divine mysteries." Her presence was responsible for the concluding prayers of the *Dialogues* and for their orientation towards the Gospels. Her contribution was frequently decisive. And so, it is not surprising that some months later, after he had gone more deeply into the teachings of Catholicism and had been regenerated by the waters of Baptism, Augustine turned once more to Monica to hear her speak of the things of God. But she was ever modest and reserved, she was a woman and lived more according to the heart than the intellect, she was a mother ready to efface herself before her son and full of admiration for him. She questioned him or expressed a wish: "What will eternal life be? How I have longed to possess it!" Augustine, questioned thus and sharing the same desire, expressed Monica's very sentiments and repeated what she had suggested in more apt, more ordered, and more startling terms. He made use of the *Enneads* and perhaps remarked: "Why not!" At Cassiciacum, she had eagerly relished a quotation from the *Hortensius* and she certainly knew that if this treatise of Cicero had recently persuaded her son to search for truth, the works of Plotinus had, to a large extent, contributed to his discovery of it. Nevertheless, she was even more pleased to hear the lofty texts from scripture which she knew well from long meditation. Above all, she enjoyed this solitude--*remoti a turbis*--which allowed her to have complete possession of the two sole objects of her love, her son and her God; she enjoyed knowing that they had finally met, and the very silence of their souls assured her that this meeting was actually taking place. Once Augustine was in contact with the supernatural and was conscious of the life of grace which came alive within him at the time of Baptism, once God had laid hold of him and he had decided to serve Him until the day of supreme recompense, he had come into complete possession of his mother's heritage. Until her death, he continued to find in her unknown treasures of grace and truth *ingenium cotidie novum*; rising with her above the sensible, Augustine, no longer the catechumen but already the neophyte, climbed to the fine point of the soul--*in se multum surrexisse*--and with her was united to God. And so the ecstasy, which was a flight toward eternity for Monica who yearned for God, meant for Augustine, who remained caught here below in time, reformation and resurrection.

CHAPTER SIX

Encounters

In primis nostra
mater, cuius meriti credo
esse omne quod vivo.
(*De beata vita,* I, 6)

Augustine's conversion should not be viewed abstractly, but rather relived imaginatively. We should recall the specific circumstances in which it took root, developed, and reached maturity. We should enter sympathetically into his successive states of soul. If we do so, we soon discover that the three elements, which exerted an influence upon his religious growth and made possible the vision at Ostia, cannot simply be classified under three general headings: Christian life, revelation, and philosophy. They were living realities, three beings of flesh and blood, Monica, Ambrose, and Simplicianus. We also come to realize that the influence of these three people was greatly increased by their cooperative effort and that their effectiveness depended upon the measure and manner in which Augustine saw them performing a sacred function and representing a social organization, the Church.

This point is clear enough in the first instance: all that hinges upon Monica and Christian life. Augustine looked upon his mother's life as the most intense and delicate, the most austere and appealing incarnation of Catholic life. They had been close for many years; he had observed her in prayer, suffering, and good works. At Cassiciacum, exterior manifestations of piety led him to suspect the treasures of her interior life. At Ostia, all doubt vanished; for he was allowed to look into the very depths of her soul and was fortunate enough to encounter the living God of Christianity in mystical union.

*

* *

Yet this vital stream of grace was transmitted to Augustine, both directly and indirectly, through other concrete agents as well as through Monica. Augustine himself assures us that he was led back to God by infectious example as well as by conviction. A soul as sensitive to human friendship, as attracted to all that was alive, as impressionable as Augustine's, could not have reacted otherwise.

The turning point in the garden at Milan is reached when Ponticianus tells the story of the two young courtiers who were converted through their reading of the life of St. Antony. Augustine remarks: "I admired these two young persons for the salutary determination with which they placed their spiritual care entirely in Your hands and the more ardently I admired them, the more detestable I found myself and the more I hated myself in comparison." This conversion was rather recent; for Ponticianus, the narrator, had known the heroes. He himself "was a practicing Christian and often remained kneeling before God in prolonged prayer." The current of ascetic life which originated in Antony's soul reached Augustine strengthened by other examples. Antony, the two young courtiers, Ponticianus, in short the entire Christian tradition, spoke to him, called to him, and encouraged him.

Augustine retired to the garden and thought about continence. Later he would write that "even at this time the voice of the flesh was growing fainter; for the chaste dignity of

Continence was revealed to me in the direction towards which I turned and where I feared to go. She stood quietly smiling without a trace of lustfulness, and invited me in a most reputable manner to come to her without hesitation. In order to receive and embrace me, she stretched forth her *holy hands, which were filled with a multitude of good examples. A host of children, maidens, countless youths, people of every age, venerable widows, women grown old in virginity*. . . . She seemed to say to me with encouraging irony: 'What? Can you not do what these women and children have done? Could they have done this by themselves and without the help of the Lord their God? It is the Lord their God who has given me to them'" (*Conf.*, VIII, 27). It would be difficult to find a better illustration of the power of example.

Thus Augustine was led by "precedent" to interpret the *Tolle lege*, the "Take and read" which he heard in the garden, as a command from heaven. At this point in his narrative, he expressly writes: "I had come to learn that as Antony happened to be reading the Gospel one day, he came upon the text, 'Go sell what thou hast, give to the poor, and thou shalt have treasure in heaven.' He eagerly interpreted these words as advice addressed to himself and was instantly converted to You by this prophecy." Prompted by Antony's example, Augustine opened the book of the Apostle at random and applied the words he came upon to himself.

Finally, the presence of his friend Alypius, a young man of chaste habits, contributed in no small way to his deliverance from impurity and to his desire for a better life. In short, Christian life was revealed to Augustine in all its attractiveness and potentiality not only through Monica, who represented for him its most authentic and perfect realization, but also through a whole chain of holy souls, and through an uninterrupted series of conversions and lives devoted to the service of God. Augustine clearly states that it was the contemporaneity and universality of Catholic life that impressed him. "Alypius and I were stunned," he writes, "to learn of your marvelous works which were accomplished in the true faith and in the Catholic Church so recently, practically in our own time. All three of us stood aghast! We, because the facts were so extraordinary; Ponticianus, because we were unaware of them. Thereafter, he talked about the great numbers who lived in monasteries, about their virtuous lives which sent up an odor of sweetness to God, and about the fruitful solitude of the wilderness. We knew nothing of all this."

Up to this time, it had been possible for Augustine to look upon Monica as a chosen soul, as an exceptional, unique, and singular creature whose ideals were consequently inaccessible to him. But now that he knew that she was but one among legions of virgins and ascetics, and now that he had been told that a community of monks lived near the walls of Milan under the patronage of Ambrose and that all of these souls aspired to Christian perfection and followed a venerable tradition, Monica's life assumed symbolic value and the power of her example new strength. Christian life was far from being the philosophy of a chosen few, it was the common property of all the faithful. Augustine, extremely affectionate and surrounded by friends since youth, became overjoyed and happy when he realized that if he were to become a convert, he would not be alone. His heart accepted the invitation.

If Augustine considered Monica the perfect symbol of Christian life and if, after having given birth according to the flesh, she had given birth to him according to the spirit, then he considered bishop Ambrose the incarnation of the apostolic tradition and one who had the authority to transmit revealed doctrine through his teaching. Once again it was not an object or an abstraction, a book or a system, but a human being who influenced Augustine and led him to conversion. While the final portion of his autobiography, as originally written, is devoted to Monica, nevertheless, Ambrose, although not explicitly mentioned, is clearly alluded to from the work's opening prayer. For according to the doctrine of St. Paul, there summarized, faith is not possible without a preacher to make it known. "Let me go in quest of You, Oh Lord," exclaims Augustine, "by calling upon You, and let me invoke You while believing in You. For You have been preached to us. This faith cries out to You, Oh Lord, this faith which You have given me, which You have inspired in me through the humanity of Your Son and through the ministry of Your Preacher." Indeed, no sooner had he arrived in Milan than he introduced himself to Ambrose. The bishop welcomed him as a father, with great charity, and from that time the pace of his conversion quickened. Ambrose's kindness certainly had an incalculable effect upon Augustine.

Augustine grew to like the bishop and listened to his sermons attentively. Charmed by the quality of Ambrose's eloquence, which he had heard praised to the skies, he hung upon his words. Later in the *Soliloquies* he would say that Ambrose was "eloquence itself--*ipsa eloquentia*" (*Sol.*, II, 26). The bishop's talent was bound to make a great impression upon the professional rhetorician. "Along with the words which I admired," he writes in the *Confessions*, "the very matters which I thought to be of small moment came into my mind. I was not able to separate them, and while I opened my heart to receive his eloquent words, gradually the truths which they contained entered as well" (*Conf.*, V, 24). Although the "spiritual" exegesis which Ambrose frequently used, and perhaps abused, did not fully satisfy Augustine at that time, it did seem capable of solving many of the difficulties which he had encountered in reading the Old Testament as a Manichaean. Augustine tells us that during this period his sect and the great Church were equal in his eyes.

When Monica rejoined Augustine in Milan, as we have seen, she did everything in her power to increase the number of conversations between Ambrose and her son and to make their contact more intimate. "She loved him," says Augustine, "as an angel of God, for she knew that it was by him that I had been brought to my present state of wavering uncertainty through which, she was firmly convinced, I would pass from sickness to health" (*Conf.*, VI, 1). Her efforts were not as successful as she would have wished. They did not see each other privately. The young man who "longed for discussion" never had the opportunity to propose his doubts and uncertainties to the bishop, still less the opportunity to debate with him in a courteous exchange of views upon questions doctrinal and scriptural. This is a rather significant point. Ambrose did not instruct Augustine in the study of his episcopal palace; he did not allow him to ask questions, raise difficulties, or make replies; he did not have a man-to-man talk with him or try to win him over; but he spoke to him as a bishop invested with a divine mandate, as the successor of the apostles, as the bearer of a message to be accepted without question. He spoke to him from the lofty ambo, from the chair of truth. The voice which Augustine came to hear each Sunday was the voice of the Church, the voice of the teaching body of the Church. Augustine was not received as a distinguished visitor; he came to his pastor with the rest of the flock. There beside Monica he listened and learned with the whole body of the Church. When the congregation prayed, he doubtless prayed with them.

Thus, as he heard Ambrose explain the scriptures and give an exposition of dogma, he gradually acquired knowledge of the Christian faith. Like most Christians, he had some grasp of the essential scriptural principles well before he began his deep study of the Old and New Testaments. And so when he opened the works of the Platonists, he was able to compare them with the holy books.

*

*   *

The preaching of Ambrose not only made certain doctrines accessible to him but, much more importantly, taught him to understand the special and unique authority that the Catholic faith attaches to the scriptures as such. As he himself remarks, it was tradition that made the inspired books intelligible to him. This is a most important page in the history of Augustine's growth and evolutions towards the faith (*Conf.*, VI, 7-8). Among his reflections of this period he notes: "I believed innumerable things which I had neither seen nor witnessed, so many events in the history of nations; so many facts about places and cities which I had never seen, I believed so many things on the word of friends, doctors, and a thousand others, and unless these reports were accepted we would be able to do absolutely nothing in this life." He then addresses himself to God and continues: "Thus You persuaded me that those who believe Your scriptures, which You have established with such great authority among nearly all nations, were not blameworthy, but rather those who did not believe them, and that I was not to listen to those who might say: 'How do you know that these books have been given to mankind by the Spirit of the true God who is Truth and Veracity Itself . . . .' Thus since our weakness has need of the authority of the holy books," he writes further on, "I began to believe that You would not have invested the scriptures with such great authority throughout the world [Augustine is alluding to the faith of the Church] unless You had wished me to believe in You and seek You through them. But as soon as I heard a satisfactory explanation of many things which I used to think absurd, I realized that my difficulties must be imputed to the profundity of their mysterious truth. Thus the authority of the scriptures seemed to me far more venerable and far more worthy of devoted faith, inasmuch as they were accessible to anyone who wished to read them, and yet reserved the imposing dignity of their mystery for a more learned interpretation. They are accessible to all through the clarity of their language and the humble simplicity of their style, and yet are capable of demanding serious application of those who are not 'frivolous.' They receive all men with open arms, but allow only a small number to come to You by the narrow way; yet this number is still larger than it would be, were it not for the prestige of their lofty authority and were they not to draw the multitude to their bosom by their holy humility." Augustine was struck once again by the notion that this multitude was the whole Catholic Church which shares in the benefits of revelation, and his contact with Ambrose allowed him to experience this phenomenon. Like the Christian life which draws nourishment from them and the Church which propounds and interprets them, the scriptures are meant for all. Augustine gave the matter serious consideration and was confident that he would not be left alone, but would remain in contact with his brothers and fellow men.

Thus Augustine was not introduced to the specifically revealed and inspired elements of the Christian religion as he was reading or as he reflected in solitude, but rather as he stood in the midst of a thick and lively crowd listening to a distinguished man, a man endowed with remarkable natural talents and extremely sympathetic towards those who approached him. As Monica and similar souls were the channels through which the life of the Church reached Augustine, so Ambrose appeared to be a bishop and nothing more, a mere spokesman of the magisterium, an echo of the voice of the Church.

*

* *

Even the influence of such a philosophy as the *Enneads* had its full effect upon Augustine's conversion only because he discovered that it had been a vital force in the life of another, indeed of a convert, only because of the human but holy authority of a worthy priest who assured him of its value and acknowledged its beneficent influence. Certainly the mere reading of Plotinus' works, especially the treatise *On the Beautiful*, had stirred Augustine's artistic and mystic soul, and had well disposed him long before this. From the very first, he was deeply impressed by the doctrine of the First Intelligence which is so similar to St. John's teaching on the Word of God. The Neoplatonic dialectic gradually led him to a transcendent and spiritual God, drew him away from Manichaeism once and for all, and removed his last philosophical obstacle to conversion. But this did not prevent Augustine from feeling the need to examine his first impressions. When he went to find Simplicianus, "who had begotten Ambrose in grace," he spoke to him not only of his moral difficulties, but also of his studies. He told Simplicianus about "all the wanderings of my errors; but when I told him that I had read certain books of the Platonists translated into Latin by Victorinus, who had once been a professor of Rhetoric in Rome and who had, so I was told, died a Christian, he congratulated me on not having chanced upon other philosophical writings which are full of error and deceit, according to the principles of this world, while the Platonists constantly introduce us to God and His Word" (*Conf*., VIII, 3). This introduction to "God and His Word" had captivated Augustine from the very first. Now an old man of vast experience and high standing in the Church confessed how happy he was that Augustine had read these works.

Encouraged by such approval, Augustine was able to devote himself to the study of the *Enneads*. In a certain sense, this work had been recommended by a theologian who was to become his friend and spiritual director. This venerable confidant certainly sensed that the time was right; his psychology was subtle and sensitive, and he had a deep respect for souls. There was no discussion; Simplicianus simply commended Augustine on his reading and told him the moving story of a beautiful and illustrious conversion. By contrasting the pretensions and proud doctrines of the Platonists with the humble and self-effacing conduct of Victorinus, their translator, Simplicianus was able to correct, or rather to complement, the impact of Plotinus upon Augustine's thought. With a charming simplicity worthy of his name, "he began to tell me about Victorinus whom he had known intimately during his stay in Rome." Once again personal contact is established, Simplicianus forges the link between his young friend and his old one, and life is again far more instructive than books. Even when this version of the *Enneads* was put into Augustine's hands, he had been told that the translator had died a Christian and his proud but secretly converted soul swelled with enthusiasm for the religion that numbered among its members such illustrious scholars. For Victorinus was indeed famous and Simplicianus did not hesitate to stress this point and quicken Augustine's interest in Catholicism. Victorinus had lived to see a statue erected in his honor in a Roman Forum and his conversion was thus all the more astonishing and thorough. He would have been permitted to make his confession of faith behind closed doors, to avoid any embarrassment, but he wished to make it in public. Simplicianus cites this as a rare example of humility and sincerity: "He lost all human respect in the face of falsehood and now could only blush before truth." And so, some years later, when the Emperor Julian ordered professors to choose between their teaching and their faith, Victorinus abandoned his chair of eloquence without hesitation or regret, "thus finding," Augustine himself remarks, "the opportunity to devote all his time to God" (*Conf.*, VIII, 10). "Now when Your servant Simplicianus had told me this story about Victorinus," Augustine concludes, "I burned with the desire to imitate him and this was exactly what Simplicianus wanted."

Thus, if the commendations of Simplicianus and a more intimate knowledge of the translator of the *Enneads* prolonged and increased the influence of their reading upon Augustine's thought, by the same token, the truly startling and moving conversion of the rhetorician-philosopher and the consecration of the last years of his life to the defense of the faith were well calculated to hasten Augustine's return to the Church. For it was the Church that was presenting and recommending Neoplatonic philosophy, if not in the guise of her spiritual leaders, at least in the person of two of her most distinguished members, Victorinus and Simplicianus. One of these was a layman, the other a cleric, both were thinkers open to the spirit and theologians of deep faith.

Therefore, the components of Augustine's religious life were not derived from mere individuals whose prudence, reputation and affection necessarily carried great weight with him, but from people who belonged to a well organized and highly developed society. Augustine was not confronted simply with a

Monica, an Ambrose, a Victorinus, or a Simplicianus, with a mother whose example was leading him on, a bishop whose words were winning him over, thinkers whose philosophy was bringing him enlightenment. No, in them and through them, the entire Catholic Church presented herself to him, with the humanism and intellectualism for which she has always been famous. In them and through them, Augustine encountered the faith of the Church received from the Apostles and deposited with her magisterium for preservation down through the ages. Above all, he was offered the seed of life that is sown in the souls of the faithful and that, when it falls upon rich ground, springs up into an abundant mystical harvest which, in turn, is scattered throughout the world in mystical charity.

*

* *

Augustine, one of these privileged souls, was born to receive great graces and to accomplish gread deeds. The Church was giving him everything and had a right to expect everything in return. She was entrusting him with all of her teachings and with her whole life that he might make this heritage bear fruit. Once Augustine became a son of the Church, he was also obliged, in a certain sense, to become her father. And so it was to be. An exchange of letters with Simplicianus--Augustine's former director and now, ten years after his conversion, his disciple--is at once a proof and a symbol of this obvious fact. In 397, both were bishops: one was the successor of Ambrose; the other, bishop of Hippo. The elder, both in age and faith, asked the opinion of the younger. Simplicianus asked Augustine to interpret seven scriptural passages, two of which are from the Epistle to the Romans, the very Epistle which had been such an important factor in Augustine's return to the Church. Augustine willingly complied and sent his colleague in Italy two volumes of commentaries entitled *De diversis quaestionibus ad Simplicianum* which he admitted are extremely long. He continued to address him as "my father" and said that he owed him this response at least in token of gratitude. Augustine commended himself to his prayers and ends his letter asking Simplicianus to forward his opinion of the work. He asked for a brief but weighty evaluation and told him that he wanted an honest opinion even though it might be severe. Although these phrases are more than mere expressions of politeness, they do not alter the fact that it is Augustine who is teaching and Simplicianus who is being instructed. Indeed, in a letter which has been lost, but which Augustine tells us he received, Simplicianus wrote that he was completely satisfied with the answers to his queries. The disciple had become the master.

If Augustine was called to become one of the great doctors of the Church, it was because the richness of his experiences, the depth of his soul, and the attractiveness of his personality formed an excellent ground for the seed of the Gospel, and because the grain of wheat sown by Monica would there yield a hundredfold. The forces that acted upon Augustine do not entirely explain either his conversion or the development which preceded or, above all, followed it. Other souls have been subjected to the influence of philosophy, have been captivated by the weight of tradition, and have sought to integrate into their lives the infinitely great and the infinitely small, and yet their development does not follow the pattern outlined in the narrative of the *Confessions*. There is but one Augustine, one scene in the garden, one vision at Ostia.

*

* *

Even before his conversion, the African rhetorician was a religious person, obsessed by the manifestations of the divine in a variety of forms. The three elements which acted upon him necessarily acted within him, and his powerful, original being reacted to them and enriched them with all that was best within him. As the Church was the exterior unifying principle offered Augustine that he might synthesize all that impressed and attracted him, so the intensity of his religious feelings and his sensitivity to the divine, clearly a special grace, was the interior structure which assimilated all the contributions of dogma, reason, and experience. If these forces exerted some creative dynamism within him and later through him, it was because they reacted within his personality as if in a magnetic field. The intensity and naturalness of this feeling forced him to believe in his individual destiny from the very outset, and to go on believing in it; it forced him to turn instinctively towards a conception of society, man, and God in which the individual is supreme.

He had always been radically convinced that he was responsible for his sins. He may have rushed into Manichaeism, a doctrine which throws all culpability for sin back upon an evil Being, largely because this feeling was so strong and because he wished to be liberated from it. Few passages in the *Confessions* better illustrate this point than the one in which he wrote: "My God, nothing in the disputes of the philosophers, whose books I had read in such abundance, was able to uproot my belief in Your existence, although Your nature was unknown to me, or to make me doubt that the government of human affairs reveals your providence. . . . I always believed that You exist and that You watch over us" (*Conf.*, VI, 7-8).

Once converted, he became even more attached to these ideas. The persons and things which struggled for his soul, such as the Platonists and the material silence of creatures at Ostia, were merely the providential instruments of divine Goodness which now called him from afar to bring him back, now lovingly inclined towards him to embrace him. Later in the *City of God* (*Civ.*, X, xiv), he returned with obvious satisfaction to that section of the *Enneads* where it is said that Providence extends even to the lowest beings and does not disdain concern for flowers, leaves, and fruit. This is at once an Evangelical and Plotinian concept. But whereas Plotinus certainly was not thinking about the One, his Absolute, when he wrote these words, but about an inferior hypostasis alone responsible for the government of the universe, Augustine remembered having read in the Gospel that Christ was interested in the lilies of the field and that the Father, who is supreme Goodness, watches over the sparrows of the Galilean skies.

The natural affinity of Augustine's soul for the most human and, at the same time, the most divine truths of Christianity constituted one of the deepest motives for his conversion. This affinity began to develop in early childhood and continued to grow strong during adolescence; for he tells us that the works in which he did not find the "sweet" name of Christ could not satisfy him. This epithet betrays a whole ambience of sympathy, a whole world of desire. The forces which acted upon him were individually quite strong, yet not at all incompatible--he could find them in the Church--and they were, according to Augustine, the sources of God's providential love. Nevertheless, such currents might not have been able to produce the mystical spark, the vision at Ostia, had they not encountered other currents hidden within the convert's soul, had not Providence prepared the field before these forces were set in motion, began to interact, and joined to form a higher synthesis.

Augustine's nostalgia for God, his desire for personal

salvation and complete possession of God, his conviction that the most perfect joy here below is but a foretaste of the future happiness he so keenly desired, all these were the very soul of his soul and the organic law of his life. The short sentence which occurs on the first page of the *Confessions*, "You have made us for Yourself and our hearts are restless until they rest in You," this *fecisti nos ad te*, is the key to Augustine's life and works.

CHAPTER SEVEN

The Syntheses

> Est ibi.
> (*Conf.*, IX, 14)

> Fecisti nos ad te et inquietum est cor nostrum donec requiescat in te.
> (*Conf.*, I, 1)

With this divine spark, this grace given Augustine, the wealth of a secular philosophy, the treasures of Church tradition, the hidden riches of Christian life came into contact. We have analysed the nature and special energy of each element. We have surely come to recognize these elements as the very ones which Augustine, in his famous description, insists to be the essential components of every religion: the institutional, the speculative, and the mystical element. We have also studied Augustine's personality, the force which activated the elements. Now we must attempt to discover the special nuances and delicate shadings of each of these religious experiences; we must try to define the laws which governed the evolution of these new syntheses.

The first flash of lightning to rip through Augustine's stormy thirtieth year was the burst of enlightenment that came with his reading of certain Platonic works; this is reflected in the contemplation at Milan like light in a fitfully luminous pool. And yet Augustine was not attracted by the charm of Plotinus' style, the brilliance of his imagery or the sublimity of his thought. Nor was he stirred by the novel and marvellous as such, by totally unfamiliar arguments, the solidity of new positions, or the magnificence of newly-revealed insights.

On the contrary, it was old, familiar things that attracted Augustine, things he had already seen or, at the very least, glimpsed. On the sense level, it was the sympathy of Plotinus for all that is beautiful, a sympathy that was profound and yet different from that of the young African aesthete; it was "the desire for God in the philosophy of Plotinus," the echo in the *Enneads* of the *fecisti nos ad te* that re-echoed in the heart of Monica's son; it was the conformity of the doctrine of the *Logos* with the Church's teaching on the *Word* as preached by Ambrose. Augustine was not surprised to discover extraordinary wisdom in Plotinus, but rather to find in a great philosopher old familiar ideas which he had had since birth, thoughts pondered at length in solitude, notions with which his mother and the bishop had quietly imbued his entire being.

Augustine does not say: "God is a spirit and must be sought in spirit and in truth," but he says: "*It was these works* that taught me to search for incorporeal truth and led me to see your invisible perfections through created things" (*Conf.*, VII, 26). He does not exclaim: "Truth, the Word, is God," but he writes: "*I read there* that the Word is God," as if he meant: "I have read in these books of the Platonists what John teaches, Ambrose preaches, and Monica believes. *Ibi legi. . .ibi legi.*" He is not content to assert: "I know that man's happiness consists in being plunged into the depths of the Word." What he does is to affirm that in reading Plotinus he actually discovered the presence of a doctrine: "that of his fullness souls receive that they may be blessed and that they are renewed by participation in his abiding wisdom that they may be wise, *is there, is truly there*" (*Conf.*, VII, 14). "*Est ibi,*" he writes, "*est ibi.*" The adverb is the emphatic word and all Augustine's enthusiasm is concentrated in it.

It would seem, therefore, that Augustine's transformation was not brought about by his reading of Plotinus, or even in the last analysis by his reconsidering the sublimity of the Johannine doctrine, but by his discovery of *this* doctrine *in Plotinus*. He felt prepared to break the attachments of the flesh not because he realized that we must go beyond the world of sense in order to reach God, but because he noticed that this requirement, which is prescribed by the Church, was also prescribed by the School. Augustine was not startled by the individual elements of the synthesis, by either Christianity or Platonism, but by their unexpected conjunction, their agreement, the synthesis itself.

*

*   *

It may be objected that we are interpreting these events according to their presentation in the *Confessions*, a work of Augustine's maturity in which he might well have blended his faith as a bishop with his convictions as a philosopher, and might have confused somewhat these two phases of his life by failing to distinguish clearly between his state of soul at the time he wrote this work and his feelings at the time of his conversion. But the synthetic and, consequently, dynamic character of the contemplation at Milan appears in the early *Dialogues* even more strikingly than it does in the *Confessions*. Here are his actual words in the treatise *On the Happy Life*. "After I had read a few books of Plotinus *and* had compared them (*conlataque*), as best I could, with the authority of those who have handed the divine mysteries down to us, I burned with enthusiasm" (*Beat.*, I, 4). The conjunction which I have italicized is as important as the adverb *there* stressed above. At this contact of stone with steel the spark leaped forth; without it nothing would have happened. *Conlataque*--everything depended upon the comparison. If further proof is needed, there is a decisive one in the *Contra Academicos,* which was written even closer to the time of these events. "When I read these books," relates Augustine, "they enkindled in me an incredible fire; it was incredible, truly incredible. I turned to that religion which had been implanted in me from infancy and which had penetrated to the very marrow of my being; indeed it was this religion which was drawing me although I knew it not. That is why trembling, impatient, but hesitating, I took up the Apostle Paul" (*Acad.,* II, ii, 5). Hardly had he perused the *Enneads* and found in them a sketch, as it were, of Christian philosophy, of certain points that are essential to the Church's thought, than he interrupted this study to return to the scriptures or, more precisely, in order to determine the accuracy of the new synthesis that had been revealed to him.

He proceeded with haste and with hesitation; for he feared that a thorough examination might not confirm his first impressions and might destroy this appealing combination of philosophy and religion. How well the following words betray Augustine's anguish and uncertainty: "trembling, impatient, but hesitating, I took up the Apostle Paul. For these men, I told myself, these Christians, would not have been able to accomplish such great things had their writings and precepts been contrary to this lofty wisdom," to this pagan wisdom! He therefore read these books very thoroughly and attentively. He began to analyse each element of the synthesis in terms of the synthesis.

All great discoveries of the human mind involve the same process. The intellect is first blinded by the total vision; it then recovers, laboriously determines the individual causes of the illumination, and submits them to a detailed examination. So it was with Augustine. As we know, he had always felt some dissatisfaction with Manichaean doctrines, and the scriptures had caused him difficulty as he had never been satisfied with literal interpretations. Only the spiritual exegesis of Ambrose had been able to dispel his doubts and begun to calm him. Now, brandishing the *Enneads* as the torch of truth, he read the scriptures in their light. Under these conditions he naturally approached this investigation with a certain amount of fear. So much depended upon this first experiment, ultimately his whole conversion. Would the synthesis stand up to analysis?

His hopes were not disappointed. He reflects in the *Confessions:* "You wished these books of the Platonists to fall into my hands before I had meditated upon your scriptures in order to preserve in my memory the impression of the effect which they had upon me. . . ." Augustine is here paying a subtle tribute to the strength and vividness of this impression. He continues: "For if I had first been formed by your sacred scriptures and had become familiar with their sweetness, and only then had I come upon these Platonic works, perhaps they would have drawn me away from the solid ground of piety, or if I had stood firm in that moral disposition, perhaps I might have thought that one could have derived equal profit from these books, had he studied them alone" (*Conf.*, VII, 26). *Etiam ex illis. . .si eos solos.* This is quite an avowal! In this same passage he openly admits that he is completely obsessed with this "lofty wisdom." Was he not tempted to employ his recently acquired knowledge, "of which he was proud," as an infallible canon of truth? The rest of the text implies as much and shows clearly the bias with which he began his study of the scriptures. The following words take up the sentence from the *Contra Academicos,* quoted just above, and complete its meaning. "And so," he continues in the *Confessions*, "I greedily seized the venerable writings of your Spirit, and above all those of the Apostle Paul. And those difficulties vanished in which he seemed to me at times to contradict himself and in which the literal meaning of his words did not seem to me to be in agreement with the testimony of the law and the prophets. I saw but one face in that chaste eloquence and I learned to rejoice with trembling. I set to work and found that whatever truth I had read in the works of the Neoplatonists was expressed here with the approbation of your grace" (*Conf.*, VII, 27). *Quidquid illac. . .hac.* What was said in the Platonic works was said here. It is a repetition of the *ibi legi.*

Thus, contrary to common opinion, he did not examine the Epistles of St. Paul at this time with the precise intention of passing judgement on the *Enneads*, still less of condemning them, but rather with the intention of applying the philosophical code of the *Enneads* to these Epistles. Christianity, however, was proved innocent of error and imperfection; it rivalled Plotinian spiritualism and even seemed superior to it. Consequently Augustine was obliged to reverse the process and to assess the comparative merits of Neoplatonism itself. Did it really have any claim to the admiration and respect of a Christian? Did it really contain, as Augustine had believed, some of the essential doctrines of Catholicism? Had the convert been the victim of some mystification? A second enquiry was imperative.

But unless he had recourse to the tribunal of the Church or consulted her through her experts and doctors, how could he know whether or not the best elements of Neoplatonism could be incorporated into a specifically religious construction, how could he decide whether the claims of this philosophy were or were not extravagant errors? This partly explains Augustine's recourse to Simplicianus, certainly one of the most prominent figures in the ecclesiastical circles of Milan, an unofficial authority, of course, but one of the best qualified and in matters of faith equivalent to a jurisconsult. They discussed, among other things, the hidden similarities between Christianity and Plotinian philosophy. Together they proceeded to weigh the evidence. "I commend you," says Simplicianus, "for having read these books which in so many ways introduce one to God and his Word." What did he mean if not that it is perfectly possible to be simultaneously a disciple of Plotinus and of Christ, but on this one condition, that the pride of Plotinus be replaced by the humility of Christ?

Simplicianus was not content to reassure his visitor about the fundamental compatibility of philosophy and revelation and in so doing to confirm his intellectual synthesis; he went on to tell him about a man, more precisely about his friend Victorinus, who had been a rhetorician, like Augustine, and who had become, as Augustine was to become a Neoplatonist philosopher and a Catholic theologian. The life and writings of Victorinus are a living proof of the harmony of the *Enneads* and Gospels. His principal work, the *Adversus Arium*, is replete with quotations from scripture and echoes of Plotinus; it is an honest attempt to explain the dogma of the Trinity with the help of notions borrowed from Neoplatonism. Yet Victorinus was also an edifying example of Christian humility, whereas the philosopher "swollen with monstrous pride," who had obtained the *Enneads* for Augustine, was for him a symbol of lofty, proud pagan wisdom.

Thus the course of Augustine's conversion shows a perfect continuity. It began when he was given a gift, an intuition which must be called a grace: Augustine perceived, as in a metageometry which he had not known before, the convergence towards infinity of two parallel vectors, of a purely rational philosophy which transcends space and time, and of a visible organization which derives from a man who lived and suffered in Palestine and died under Tiberius, that is, from Jesus Christ. This synthesis was revealed in a simple and original act of vision and as such cannot be broken up. From this unexpected and gratuitous event--"For it is you," Augustine says to God, "who procured these Platonic works for me"--the stages followed one after the other with inescapable logic.

Conversion is a serious matter and requires an effort of the intelligence as well as a loving submission of the will. The risk of eternity and salvation is no game. No one accepts indiscriminately a faith which involves the whole person, which imperiously demands the submission of all faculties, the mind as well as the heart. This is why Augustine plunged into his study of the scriptures. He had to find out whether they would give way beneath the weight of this philosophy, whether the vision was only a mirage, whether he could truly believe with Ambrose and think with Plotinus.

As has so well been said, this question gives rise to the first crisis over matters of belief in the mind of the Christian, the adolescent crisis. The child who wakes to the life of the senses and casts a glance of unaffected surprise over the world accepts Christianity as a wonderful, consoling story, and the Church as a large family that speaks to him with the authority of a father and for whose honor men are willing to shed their last drop of blood. The paladins of this romance died "martyrs" for their "confession" of Christ, the head of the family, or for their refusal to betray the sacred scriptures, the sacred patrimony which perpetuates his memory and prolongs his activity. In the child's religion, it is the traditional element that predominates.

The young man experiencing the upsurge of his intellect wants proof for things which he had previously accepted without question. Revolting against the yoke of family tradition, he begins to question what he formerly obeyed as a precept handed down by his forefathers. If, in his opinion, his present principles do not happen to justify these imperious commands, if the strong acid of his theorizing utterly effaces the attraction of the enchanting pictures of childhood, if he is incapable of reconciling organized religious belief and independent personal reasoning, he will either shut himself up in desperation with the former, so as to take refuge in a species of pleasant superstition and become a parasite on the faith, or else, intoxicated by the philosophy of early manhood, he will leave his paternal home and set out to wander through the world of emancipated reason. For all religion, far from being something simple and isolated, is complex and all-embracing, and if the balance is destroyed it engenders, under one form or another, revolt or apostasy.

As apostasy is the dissolution of the constitutive elements of religion, so conversion is the integration of previously dissociated elements. Well before his conversion, Augustine possessed a philosophy and was familiar with Christ. The *Hortensius* had shown him that happiness could be found in the pursuit of truth. His mother, then Ambrose, had taught him that Christianity is a source of light for the intellect and peace for the heart. Still, he did not become a convert. The elements remained isolated: Manichaean materialism declared itself incompatible with Christian beliefs. However, should another philosophy with a spiritual foundation reveal itself through an elaboration of the ideas implied in the *Hortensius* and, above all, parallel the doctrine of St. John and St. Paul, and should this synthesis become possible, then conversion will not be far off. Augustine saw this possibility in a flash and at once began to search for a way to bring it about. By making a comparative study he tried to determine whether or not traditional doctrine--*divina mysteria tradiderunt*--satisfied the intellectual demands which Plotinus, and through him philosophy itself, made known to him; then, when this inquiry had been brought to a favourable conclusion, he tried to determine whether or not the rational positions of Neoplatonism could be reconciled with the unyielding dogmas of the Church: *in istis insinuari Deum et eius Verbum*. This comparative method brought him back to his initial inspiration. At about this time occurred the contemplation at Milan, the final synthesis of this first and essential phase of his conversion. We would not venture to hold that it happened any earlier, and would rather believe that it took place after the interview with Simplicianus. Indeed, from the very nature of the analyses which preceded and engendered it, this contemplation was intellectual and intellectualistic, and yet it was also religious; for it arose from the confluence of two streams which had previously flowed in separate channels--they came together at this point and swept Augustine towards the Christian faith.

It is still possible to distinguish between the Christian spirit of the ecstatic description of the contemplation at Milan and the Plotinian conception and vocabulary used to express it. There is, in fact, as Augustine and Simplicianus recognized, a world of difference between the *Logos* of the *Enneads* and the *Incarnate Word* of the Johannine Prologue, between the presumption of the pagan philosopher and the humble acknowledgement of the Christian. Nevertheless, since it is still the same man and the whole man who believes, thinks, loves, and speaks through different faculties, these elements reacted strongly upon each other. Consequently, these candid pages are no more the work of a Christian tinged with Platonism than of a Platonist tinged with Christianity. Although the contemplation at Milan is essentially Plotinian, it is already truly Catholic. It is the experience of a philosopher who is becoming a believer, or rather of a former believer who is returning to the faith without ceasing to be a philosopher.

If thoroughgoing religion calls not simply for a set of external practices nor even a ritualistic life sustained and nourished by mystical life, but also implies a doctrine, a faith that is addressed to the intellect, we must not be surprised to find that even though the vision at Milan was religious, it was still a highly intellectual experience. As a matter of fact, it was primarily intellectual. As the convert himself admits, he reflected a great deal more during this period than he prayed. If the language of the *Confessions* is here more metaphysical than biblical, if whole sections are decidedly speculative in character, it is a proof of their author's sincerity and an indication that Augustine was in earnest about his return to God, that he returned fully and frankly, soul and intellect, heart and mind.

*
* *

Even during this first crisis the third universal element of religion, the mystical element, was at work. This seems to be one of the characteristics which distinguish Augustine's conversion from all others. The ecstasy at Milan began, if we may so put it, with a search after God for himself alone. The special grace given Augustine, analysed above, played a fundamental role. We speak constantly of his intellectual development, we trace his conversion to an illumination of his discursive faculties, and we neglect the emotional and unifying aspect of this evolution. The course of Augustine's intellectual crisis of faith was marked by deep mystical yearnings for God.

Augustine was a born mystic. Moreover, he inherited this gift: his mother was also a mystic. It was this natural appetite for God, this hunger and thirst for union, that prevented him from feeling at home with Manichaean doctrine and explain his sense of interior liberation when he read the *Enneads*. The spirituality of God occupied a pre-eminent place in his strictly intellectual evolution, because although it is certainly possible to found a sufficiently coherent philosophical system upon materialism or dualism--witness Stoicism and Manichaeism--a mystic can only be a spiritualist and a monist. This seems to be the reason why Augustine's conversion was not possible as long as he remained bound to the doctrines of Mani; this is why once these fetters had fallen from him and the spirituality of God was clear to him, his soul took flight and, giving rein to its instinct, soon reached a high form of contemplation. Here we have a new and possibly the most profound reason for Augustine's enthusiasm for the *Enneads*. This work is not merely the fruit of philosophical thought; some of its pages show it to be a testimony of one "who has seen." In the treatise *On the Beautiful* in particular, and there more frequently than elsewhere, Plotinus makes discreet allusions to his own mystical experiences: "He who has seen," he writes, "knows what I mean" (*Enn.*, I, 6, 7). Such references must have moved Augustine as much as the intellectual achievements of the treatise must have convinced him. If Augustine was to be himself, he had to believe in the existence of a spiritual Beauty and a spiritual Goodness. Plotinus, a philosopher and a visionary, presented him with this ideal as a postulate of reason; he was vouching, as a thinker, for the true worth of those mystical tendencies which were sweeping Augustine along although he knew it not.

In Plotinus the dialectic leads to union. "There are two paths," he says, "for those who climb and soar; the first way is from below; the second is the path of those who have already attained the world of ideas and have, to some degree, established a footing there; they should advance to the farthest limits of this world; the moment at which they reach the summit of the intelligible marks the end of the journey" (*Enn.*, I, 3, 1). In the philosophy of the *Enneads*, the second of these paths is only a prolongation of the first. Philosophy goes beyond itself and is completed in ecstasy. The path followed by the Intelligence leads into the unified contemplation of the One. Thus one of the constitutive elements of the vision at Milan, one of the prime factors in Augustine's first crisis, indeed the most important one since we call it an intellectual crisis, was tinged with mysticism.

I do not maintain that Augustine consciously sought mystical experience; on the contrary, he was struggling with difficulties on the philosophical level and was searching for an answer in a system rather than in a way of life. In extraordinary people, however, act goes beyond intent and life reaches out far beyond consciousness. In a very true sense they do, for good or for evil, what they do not wish to do, or rather what they think they do not wish to do. For the insatiable appetite for being is ever awake within them, an appetite that is as infinite as being itself and urges them on at every step. It is this nostalgia for God, this deep-rooted love of the divine, which permeates Augustine's most philosophical meditations.

*

* *

The same mystical tone which had captivated the young Augustine in the *Enneads* of Plotinus appeared again in the second element of his first religious synthesis, the scriptures and tradition. For some time he had tried unsuccessfully to appreciate the scriptures: in his youth he had been repelled by their simple style; later the crude interpretations which he was given involved the texts in apparent contradictions. Only after hearing Ambrose did he begin to reconsider his rhetorical and philosophical biases. And he did so because Ambrose had taught him to discover the spiritual meaning behind the words of scripture and, following a venerable tradition begun by Philo and resumed by the Christian Origen, had made him read the scriptures not as a rhetorician or as a philosopher--as he had claimed to do up to this time--but as a mystic.

Just as the doctrinal sources of the contemplation at Milan must be sought, on the philosophical side, in those treatises of Plotinus in which mysticism is near the surface, so, on the scriptural side, Augustine drew inspiration chiefly from the most mystical of the sacred authors or from those passages which describe extraordinary states of soul. In the Old Testament, for example, there were the words which God spoke to Moses from the burning bush: "I am Who Am" (*Conf.*, VII, 16). In the New Testament, there were the Prologue of St. John's Gospel and (there are three references to this) the revelation of the invisible world through the visible, which St. Paul announced to the Romans. Thus, in this synthesis of organized religious belief and philosophical thought, the elements of mysticism, which are to be found in each component and which pervade Augustine's total being, act as a catalytic agent, drawing the components together and contributing to their reaction. But even though this third factor was as active as the other two, it did not appear in the new compound. Augusting was not conscious of all that was happening in the recesses of his soul. He considered himself a philosopher, whereas he was primarily a mystic. In the abstract language of the Schools, we may say that the contemplation at Milan was "formally" intellectual but "virtually" mystical. But in fact it was religious.

These constitutive factors had no more chance of being independent of one another than religion has of being purely ritualistic, or purely dogmatic, or purely experiential. The synthesis is entirely present in each part of the whole. Everything in the Church is holy, the objects of worship as well as the articles of the Creed, the breast of the first-communicant and the forehead of the dying, the hands of the priest and the definitions of the Councils. Holy also are the insights of the theologians, though they are not on a par with the voice of the bishops or with the life of the faithful. From the moment of conversion, that is to say when a soul turns towards God, everything becomes sacramental. Everything that is genuinely religious has about it something of a concrete symbol or objective guarantee, some doctrinal meaning or mystical richness.

But even though each of the three universal elements of religion is always present with the other two, a man does not have to be aware of this presence; it may be real but latent. Men are strangely deluded about the motives for their actions. Most frequently they are ignorant both of their causes and their consequences. So too, this spiritual radiation is revealed only with time, when the element has spent itself and ceases to act. Often enough we do not grasp the thesis of a book until we have read the last page.

This is why Augustine had first to reach the vision at Ostia and to survey the past from its heights before he could see the majestic contour of the contemplation of Milan in all its grandeur. Augustine was trying to conquer this peak from every side. Guided by Ambrose, he advanced along the road of the scriptures and tradition, then he left this road, turned back, hesitated, and sought his way in the steps of Plotinus. Urged on by some unknown force, he occasionally rushed forward blindly along the path of mysticism. Later he rejoined the beaten tracks of philosophy and authority and, taking these short cuts from one track to the other, he climbed and climbed. When at last he reached a great height, and saw that these two tracks--for he could not see the short cuts--opened out upon the same panorama and that as the months had gone by he had been climbing the slopes of the holy mountain from which the Lord, the God of philosophers and the God of Christians, had been summoning the pilgrim of truth throughout his journey: *Clamasti de longinquo* (*Conf.*, VII, 16).

*

*   *

Although all doubt was banished, the conflict between faith and reason settled, and Augustine's mind convinced, the powers of his will had only been thrown into confusion and continued to resist the attraction of grace. Although he had climbed so high, Augustine still found himself far from God, "in a region of strangeness--*regione dissimilitudinis*--where I seemed to hear Your voice from on high: 'I am,' You were saying, 'the food of the strong; believe and you shall eat Me'" (*Conf.*, VII, 16). He testified that, "in the flash of a trembling glance I attained Being itself, but I was not strong enough to fix my gaze upon it, and when I was beaten back again in my weakness and returned to my usual state, I brought away with me nothing except a loving memory which yearned for the aroma, as it were, of the banquet which I was as yet unable to eat." Having cited this text, we should call attention to the transition of metaphors from those of sight to those of taste; the former are more suitable for the expression of an intellectual conviction; the latter for the expression of a mystical state. "I sought," he continues, "a way to acquire the strength that would allow me to enjoy You, and I could not find it until I had embraced the Mediator between God and man,

Jesus Christ, who is above all things, God forever blessed, He who calls to us and says: 'I am the Way, the Truth, and the Life," He who mingled with our flesh that food which I was too weak to take. For the Word was made flesh, that in our infancy we might be suckled by Your wisdom, that wisdom by which You created all things" (*Conf*., VII, 24). No, he was not yet humble enough to possess Jesus, who is humility itself, and he did not yet have a soul that was childlike enough and a heart that was pure enough to see God. Even after he had read the *Enneads* in the light of the Gospel, his pride and animal passions still kept him far from the port--*uxoris honorisque inlecebra detinebar* (*Beat.*, I, 4).

Before Augustine could make his final ascent these bonds had to be broken, the powers of affection which subtend all mysticism had to be turned away from sensual beauty and directed towards the joy of ecstasy. The education of the heart is progressive, like all other types of education, and the intellect has its place in it. Although Augustine's first religious synthesis, the philosophico-dogmatic one, did not break all his bonds at a single blow, it did wear them down. During the months that followed the contemplation at Milan, each of its constitutive elements prepared him for liberation. Plotinus calmly and firmly recommended flight from the world of the senses to another world, taught him to look down on corporeal beauty, and urged perfect detachment. St. Paul preached the same principles in his own vehement and impassioned way. Reason and authority, not content to converge upon the same point in the realm of speculative thought, blended their beams and insisted upon the same renunciations. But if these beacons gave light, they were still, especially that of philosophy, without heat. Although the intellect can find delight in abstract and universal forms, the will is awakened only by contact with concrete being. Love wishes to possess a person and to be possessed in return.

Then, in the morning of his life, through the slowly-lifting haze of the scriptures, Augustine saw the towering figure of Christ gradually appear upon the horizon surrounded with all the splendour of His divinity. Even then, he recalled, "I recognized Him to be a perfect man, a real man whom I thought should be preferred above all others, not as Truth personified, but because of the extraordinary excellence of His human nature and His more perfect participation in wisdom." But it was at this juncture that "breaking with the delusive errors" of the heretics who denied the divinity of Christ, he finally understood the "sacrament" contained in the words "*the Word was made flesh*" (*Conf.*, VII, 25), and knew that Jesus, who was not only born of the Virgin and truly man but also "true God of true God" as the Nicene Creed declares, would alone be able to satisfy him, and that in Him alone would he find the fulfilment of all his powers of love.

Therefore we should not talk about a purely intellectual or even, as some have called it, a purely moral conversion. Such a conversion, devoid of any religious and mystical experience, would be a conversion only from the psychological point of view and, especially when it involves a soul as passionate as Augustine's, would be a sort of literary fiction, the product of a bookish erudition that is insensitive to the ways of life. It is not at all likely that Augustine would have been able to tear himself away from the embraces of a woman with whom he had lived for a dozen years, whom he loved, and whose son he adored, in order to embrace a mere abstraction, a mere philosophical theory, beautiful and lofty though it may have been. Augustine's exquisite sensibility could not remain without an object but, when his higher intuitive faculties became active and started to exert an influence upon him, Christ alone could satisfy his great need for love. Christ led to the

Father and was supremely lovable in himself: He was the Way, the Truth, and the Life.

Attractive though this Way was to Augustine, he "still did not feel courageous enough to follow its narrow course" (*Conf.*, VIII, 1). He wavered between these two ways of life and these two loves; his being was torn in two directions. The mind that Christian humility had not yet made submissive to God was now conscious of the revolt of the senses. "Until then I imagined that I put off from day to day contempt for worldly hopes in order to bind myself to God, only because I did not see any certain light that would orient my course. But the day would come when I would find myself bare before the reproaches of my conscience" (*Conf.*, VIII, 18). Christ was attracting him, but the flesh was holding him back. But one by one the contagion of example and a mysterious call that was at once from within and from without were to break down the last show of resistance on the part of his dual--animal and spiritual--nature.

There was inspiration in the humility of Victorinus the rhetorician, the devotion of Ponticianus, the austerities of Antony of Egypt, the ardor with which two young courtiers at Trier became converts, the monastic life of the brothers at Milan, and finally that long line of virgins and ascetics who had given themselves to God in perfect chastity. All these people were made of flesh like himself. Several of them were his contemporaries, just as young and ardent as himself, but they had outstripped him and were generously following in the footsteps of Christ. They made him feel ashamed and urged him to follow them. If in spite of everything he remained undecided, it was because a soul as fundamentally mystical as his could not give itself by halves. God was demanding a holocaust.

While Augustine's bewilderment only increased with each

moment as Ponticianus told his story and while the crisis was reaching its climax in the garden where he had retired with Alypius, it took but a child's ditty, a few verses from St. Paul--in themselves insignificant trifles, as is so often the case--to put a quick end to it all and shift his life abruptly from one love to the other. The mystical forces within him were liberated. If a grain of sand was sufficient to sway the balance decisively, it was because the already heavily weighted scale of grace was ready to tip downward, and because Augustine attached enormous importance to these trifles. As he had faith in Providence and as his ear was turned towards God, he thought he heard a voice from heaven in this child's voice; he opened the book of the Apostle like someone consulting a collection of oracles to solve an inextricable problem and make a decision. "Take and read! Take and read!" He therefore took the book, opened it, and read quietly the first passage that met his eyes: "Do not spend your life in rioting and drunkenness, not in chambering and impurities, not in contention and envy, but put on the Lord Jesus Christ and make not provision for the flesh in its concupiscences." Scarcely had he finished these lines when certainty and light illumined his heart and banished every shadow of doubt (*Conf.*, VIII, 29). He decided to renounce marriage and live for God alone. The text of the Epistle to the Romans is certainly not directly concerned with the question of continence or perfect chastity; Augustine gave these words a meaning they do not have. This should not puzzle anyone, unless he has no understanding of those secret attractions which influence the movements of the soul, or of that extremely subtle and delicate action called grace, unless he has shut his eyes to the deep-seated tendencies of this convert whose heart was made for God and was restless until it rested in Him. Augustine, then, read into this text what he was looking for; he approached it with a prejudice, yes, with a religious prejudice; he read it in the light of a rich synthesis of dogma and philosophy, reason and tradition; he saw his own special vocation imaged in it. He found there along with an exhortation to abandon the pleasures of the flesh--the negative and liberating aspect of the case--an invitation to put on Christ mystically--the positive aspect, satisfying and perfective, and attracting him as a magnet attracts iron.

*

* *

Such is the first section of the road that links the contemplation at Milan to the vision at Ostia. Just as before the contemplation at Milan there had been for his mind to work upon a salutary philosophical scepticism and a spiritual doctrine which made possible and facilitated the synthesis of faith and reason, so also, before the vision at Ostia, a long preparation was necessary to liberate his heart and set his mystical faculties consciously and deliberately in motion. The scene in the garden constituted the most outstanding, but not the final episode of this preparation. It completed a period of incubation which brought forth love, though the education of the heart would continue. The fires of the senses were extinguished and the smoke of pride dispelled. Henceforth the way would be open; for no one approaches God unless he is immaculate, chaste in body and pure of spirit: *Beati mundo corde quoniam ipsi Deum videbunt*. But no eye can gaze upon the sun unless it has become like the sun; divine grace is necessary if we are to see God.

Week after week, throughout all Advent and Lent, he lived on this nourishment, reflecting on past experiences, instructing himself under the guidance of Monica and Ambrose, meditating upon the scriptures, and praying with the psalmist to the

God towards whom he was hastening. When he left the retirement of the desert, there was the joy of Baptism, the outpouring of the Holy Spirit and the surge of divine life within his soul. He was treading the ground of the sacred foothills and he may have thought that he had arrived at his destination. But then these words of Jahweh were addressed to himself: "What are you doing here? Go forth and stand upon the mount before the Lord. And behold the Lord passes, and a great and strong wind before the Lord overthrowing the mountains and breaking the rocks to pieces: the Lord is not in the wind. And after the wind an earthquake; the Lord is not in the earthquake. And after the earthquake a fire; the Lord is not in the fire. And after the fire a whistling of a gentle air. And when he heard it, he covered his face with his mantle, and coming forth stood at the entrance to the cave, and behold a voice spoke to him. . . ." (III *Kings*, xix).

Here, at last, is the full religious experience in which the earlier synthesis of faith and reason is incorporated into a higher synthesis and is fused with life and love. We recall that for a religious being, for one at least who attains full development, there are normally two crises: the first at the end of adolescence when traditional notions are confronted with the demands of independent thinking; the second and more formidable crisis at the period of maturity when a new mystical leaven is mixed with the azyme. This is the critical moment. If the action of the leaven is not hindered, the soul will soon be able to nourish itself with a perfect bread, that is, with a religion that lacks nothing: neither facts, dogmas, nor rites, which satisfy our need to accept, believe, and act; nor the intellectual systematization and theological coherence, which satisfy our need to think and understand; nor the mysterious consciousness of a participation in the divine life, which satisfies our need for love.

Such, indeed, was the vision at Ostia. We should now understand how it resembles and differs from the contemplation at Milan. Both are religious experiences, not only philosophical or mystical but specifically religious; for in successive syntheses both integrate those elements which when united constitute the perfect essence of religion. On both occasions, Augustine took a decisive step towards God, at Milan under the influence of Ambrose and the direction of Simplicianus, at Ostia hand in hand with his mother Monica. Both are anticipated by a period of confusion during which the elements are disposed and adapt themselves slowly to the exigencies of the approaching synthesis; both are inaugurated by personal contact with souls, with living beings, by the attraction of a great social body.

Although these experiences are so similar, one is not a repetition of the other. The contemplation at Milan is more intellectual and, because the emphasis is on the speculative side, the language which describes it will naturally be more metaphysical and the vocabulary and conception will recall the *Enneads*; but because the element that is joined with philosophy is revelation and because the religion which informs the higher synthesis is Christianity, the spirit of the contemplation at Milan will be totally Christian. By the mere presence of a woman the vision at Ostia has a more emotional character. Here, although the conception is still Plotinian, the vocabulary is less so; for Monica and Augustine will prefer to look to the scriptures, though not exclusively, for adequate expression of the supernatural life of the soul and of a mind not only Christian by mystic.

The mystical leaven was present from the very start, facilitating at Milan, for example, the kneading together of dogma and philosophy; then its activity increased as the warming influence of Christ caressed the soul of the convert until it suddenly assumed full strength and made all the dough rise in an instant--*et est fermentatum totum.* Far from suppressing the other elements, the mystical element permeated them so intimately that they can no longer be dissociated. Of course a laboratory technician could approach his study of the vision at Ostia with the aid of balances and test-tubes, could analyze it and could establish, as far as weight goes, that only a negligible quantity of the mystical element was present; he might be an excellent chemist, he might measure the number and the cadences of Augustine's periods with great exactness, he might even appreciate the choice of words and the brilliance of the imagery, he might list all the scriptural allusions and discover even the slightest reminiscence of the *Enneads*; but if his senses are dull he will not perceive the exquisite aroma and delicate taste of this mystical nourishment. The profound meaning of the vision at Ostia will remain hidden from him.

In this ecstasy Augustine attained the perfection of Christian life, in so far as it is possible here below. The rapidity of this transformation and its thoroughgoing effects certainly make it an extraordinary phenomenon. Because of it, this conversion, which clearly obeyed the universal laws of religious psychology, obviously retains its individuality, and stands as a unique experience of supereminent value, the secret of which must be sought in the excellence of the special grace given the convert.

Even in his childhood, then later in the early years of manhood, there is clear evidence of a personal religious instinct and a passionate desire for truth. Like those torrents that plunge beneath the earth only to come to the surface further along still wider and deeper, these tendencies could disappear for a time, but they were not to be lost. At the appointed time, Augustine passed victoriously through two religious crises and recovered first the faith and then the fullness of the life of faith. In a few months, he passed through stages of the journey which less favoured souls take many years to traverse or which remain forever impassable to them. Almost without a break, he passed from spiritual youth to spiritual maturity. No sooner had Christianity, the beautiful *romance* of his youthful imagination, become a *doctrine* for his mind than his mature heart at once discovered in it a rich and vibrant *life*.

CHAPTER EIGHT

THE LEAVEN

> μακαριος οψιν μακαριαν τεθεαμενος.
>
> (*Enn.*, I, 6, 7)

> si continuetur hoc. . . ut talis sit sempiterna vita quale fuit hoc momentum intellegentiae. . . . nonne hoc est: *intra in gaudium domini tui?*
>
> (*Conf.*, IX, 25)

Monica died, her mission accomplished, and Augustine found himself alone in the world with God. While his mother lived, he had climbed steadily towards this summit, the vision at Ostia, and had been preparing himself for the service of the Most High. Now that he had come down, his duty was clear, he would bear witness to God.

Heresy was raging around him. The previous year, he had actually seen Ambrose shut himself up in his cathedral with his faithful in order to resist the Arians and the pressure of Justina, the young emperor's mother. Augustine was only a recent convert, but in the solitude of Cassiciacum he dreamed of strengthening the members of the Church in their faith and of leading his old friends, the Manichaeans, back to the right path. He was too generous not to share his rediscovered wealth of knowledge. He remained in Rome a few months longer and began to write a comparative study of the Catholic and Manichaean way of life. The work was written in the same form as the *Opuscula* which would later be completed in Africa. Prior to his conversion, Augustine had published only a brief, rather unimportant essay on aesthetics, but from his conversion until the *Retractationes,* he was unable to lift pen from paper. No sooner did he return to the bosom of the Church than his talent as a writer blossomed forth and for the rest of his life, nearly half a century, he would sustain intensive production. His conversion liberated not only his body, his soul, and his mind, but his literary abilities as well. He did not find himself completely until he found himself in the Church again. As catechumen, neophyte, priest, and bishop, Augustine did little more than utilize the extraordinary richness of the experiences of his thirtieth year. Because his conversion, which necessarily includes the vision at Ostia, was a complete religious experience, it reveals the origin and psychology of numerous doctrines which would later form an essential part of his philosophy and theology.

*

* *

Men who are temperamentally like Augustine generally reach the peak of their creativity between the ages of thirty and forty. This is their most fruitful time of life, not necessarily in terms of literary production and external activity, but in thoughts and desires. For the rest of his life, such a man usually does little more than coin the treasure amassed during these years: the massive ingots, long held in reserve, are converted into ready cash and common coin. And the more deeply such material lies buried within a man, the more he must struggle to bring it forth. The thinker depends less upon the external world and lives more within himself than the man of action: he nourishes himself with his own substance.

However, no intellectual discipline has a more intimate object than metaphysics or religious philosophy. For the mind is the faculty of being and God reveals Himself to man more through the soul than through the revolution of the celestial spheres. All philosophies, great and small, are only sublimations of life: in the crucible of the intellect, which naturally tends to generalize, the vital, highly individualized compounds are purified and assume universal value. As its name indicates, metaphysics is an effort to transport concrete, unique, irreversible duration from time to eternity. Despite its claims, metaphysics, like every science, is only a quantification of qualitative data, but it is a quantification of a superior order. In short, metaphysics is only a translation of a psychological state into symbols and it must be so if such a state is to be communicated to others. When metaphysics adopts the symbolism of the poet, it is expressed in imagery; when it adopts the symbolism of the scholar, it is developed in a series of propositions.

The choice of form, however, is not entirely arbitrary. To speak only of religious philosophy, should the philosopher wish to stress the institutional, intellectual, or mystical element, he would use either contemporary language, the technical expressions of some sort of scholasticism, or any one of a variety of hermetic systems. Thus common sense, reasoned discourse, or intuition may dominate the expression, but the primary and fundamental impression, the radical experience to be translated into symbols will always be predominantly intuitive.

This is why the so-called philosophies of intuition--Augustine's among them--show the least discrepancy between observed reality and its verbal communication, appear more satisfying, and enjoy an understandable success. The same may be said of religion. From the very beginnings of Christianity a dogma as essential as belief in the Trinity has been revealed principally through devotion. St. Paul, for example, sets it forth much more frequently when the occasion calls for advice than when it calls for instruction. This does not mean that dogma is subordinate to morality, but it does mean that dogma is often more adequately expressed in devotion and in a way of life than in words.

*
* *

Because the soul and life are the true objects of thought, there are, in a sense, no philosophies, there are only philosophers. A discipline does not prosper, a body of doctrine is not enriched by the constant reedition of the same material, by the transmission of the same themes under different names from textbook to textbook, from generation to generation. Far from being an indication of continuous growth, such repetition is rather the sign of irremediable decline. If there is a *philosophia perennis,* it exists in spite of the textbooks, and not thanks to them. If the human race can hope for any development of tradition, for any certain and very real perpetuity of thought, it is, as Plotinus would have expressed it, because souls have one and the same Father, from whom they come and to whom they return, because minds are of the same lineage, because men are united, whether they like it or not, to attain the same end, and because this end, true to the general law of life and movement, draws all their interior inclinations and relentlessly directs the sequence of their activities. But in virtue of this same law, inactivity antecedent to fruition is fatal: the cessation of life is death. A developing organism, even one merely content to preserve good health and maintain the status quo, eliminates used, harmful tissues, absorbs and assimilates new material. Should it give up the struggle for continual rejuvenation, should it lose the will to live, it goes into decline and sooner or later dies. Augustine served the Church in an extraordinary way, not only by enriching the common treasury of the faithful with the wealth of his own existence, but also by integrating the philosophy of Plotinus with Christian thought and by adapting it to express dogma and even mystical life. By introducing so-called "foreign" elements into the religion of his childhood, he certainly did not corrupt it; rather he contributed to its growth and did his part to help it reach maturity. This diligent servant of the Gospels did not allow the talents entrusted to him to remain unproductive.

The heritage left by Augustine is extraordinarily important; for the ground which he unremittingly cultivated during his lifetime was unusually fertile. Suffering had cleared the land of brambles and thorns, the soil was rich and fine and had been improved by various deposits. It yielded a hundredfold. This field was Augustine's life and he gathered its prodigious golden harvest into his vast "memory." He threshed the quivering sheafs of experience with the flail of his vigorous intellect, then he kneaded the fine wheat flour within his soul and, under the influence of the mystical leaven added by the vision at Ostia, the dough rose. While he lived, he shared this nourishing doctrine and life with the multitudes, but he also placed it in the vast storehouse of his works for future generations. Centuries have not yet emptied it and all Christians, both learned and unlearned, are still drawing nourishment from this harvest. If we are attracted to Augustine's works, as were antiquity and the Middle Ages, it is because they are deeply rooted in life and because we still sense in them the humble, strong odor of our poor human clay; it is also because they matured under the sun of grace and retain an infinitely delicate flavor, a taste both mystical and divine.

They satisfy all of mankind's religious needs, because the religion which they explain is a true religion, a religion at once revealed, understood, and lived.

*

* *

It would be quite valuable to show how Augustine's life, particularly what he did and thought just before and after his conversion, permeates all his teaching, and thus to interpret his great dogmatic treatises in the light of the *Confessions*. The Word, that Interior Master who occupies an eminent place in Augustine's theory of knowledge, had been revealed to him at Milan both by Plotinus the philosopher and St. John the Apostle. He came upon the first explanation of original sin in the Epistle to the Romans which he had with him "in the garden" and this formidable problem was to occupy the second part of his career. Perhaps he also discovered a remote analogy with original sin in the Neoplatonic theory of the fall of souls as proposed by Origen and Plotinus, but above all he knew from experience the weakness of the will and the sway of the passions. Augustine had experienced the effects of concupiscence within himself, he had personally suffered the consequences of Adam's sin and may even have exaggerated them. For the Church does not follow him without reservation on this point. His well-known formulation of the dogma of the Trinity is psychological and Augustine, as more than one Greek Father of the Church, drew it from the famous treatise of Plotinus *On the Three Hypostases* and other similar works; for nothing prevented him from adapting them to meet the demands of faith.

The Incarnation, however, is the central dogma upon which all others depend, the dogma of the Trinity as well as the dogmas of original sin, redemption, the sacraments, and the Church;

Augustine states that he did not find the slightest hint of the dogma of the Incarnation in the *Enneads*. Nothing resembling it, no yearning for it: *ibi non est*. Belief in the Incarnate Word is proportionate to desire for His grace. "None of this is to be found in the works of Platonists," he writes. "These pages show us nothing of the countenance of piety, the tears of confession, the sacrifice which You love, the tribulations of the spirit, the contrite and humbled heart; they show us neither the salvation of Your people nor the espoused city, neither the promise of the Holy Spirit nor the chalice of our redemption. In these pages no one sings: 'Shall not my soul be submitted to God? From Him is my salvation; for He is my God, my salvation, and my defense: I shall be no more moved.' In these pages no one hears the call: 'Come unto me, all you who labor.' They scorned these lessons because He is meek and humble of heart. For You have hidden these things from the wise and prudent and revealed them to the little ones" (*Conf.*, VII, 27). Augustine had heard this call; for he suffered in both spirit and flesh. He had answered it with all his being, immolating his flesh, humiliating his spirit. He preserved an unfading memory of his dialogue with Jesus and merited the title Doctor of Grace, only because Christ first deigned to make him the Convert of Grace. The richness of his teaching seems to be derived totally and directly from his soul.

*

* *

We cannot stop to trace the development of these vital contributions throughout all of Augustine's philosophical and theological works, but we can at least follow the maturation of the doctrines connected with the vision at Ostia. Therefore, let us leave aside the general quality of intense mysticism which colors all of the convert's teaching and focus deliberately upon the central and essential mysticism of this vision. Monica, as we know, was speaking with her son about heaven. She had the feeling that she was soon to be called to heaven and brought up the subject. The problem of happiness, discussed at length at Cassiciacum, came up again. Shortly before, while talking with his friends as a Christian philosopher, Augustine had said that happiness consisted in the perfect knowledge of God and made it clear that such happiness was within man's reach here below. Even at this time, as we recall, Monica had intervened. As far as she was concerned, only faith, hope, and charity could lead man to the happy life which is reserved for the blessed in heaven. It is remarkable that in the *Retractationes*, Augustine would later take back and correct the conclusion of the *De beata vita*. He would regret not having said that only the afterlife can be a life of happiness, and that man cannot know and, a fortiori, cannot enjoy God perfectly here below. Thus he came around to Monica's own position and rather quickly too; for this realization dates from the vision at Ostia. The mystic corrected the philosopher's doctrine, experience enlightened his intelligence. Knowledge of God is not sufficient for happiness, possession is also necessary.

Now such possession is emphatically conceived in terms of the joy Augustine experienced in the vision at Ostia. "Let us suppose that this moment of understanding were to continue, would this not be eternal life?" This strange reflection seems to have originated with the son, not the mother. Is the only difference between Augustine's rapture at Ostia and the happiness of the blessed who see God face to face the fact that the blessed have the assurance that their vision will continue forever, while Augustine's was quickly ephemeral and fleeting?

If so, it is an excellent confirmation of the thesis that, for Augustine, the height of mystical contemplation lies in an obscure, but genuine and strictly intuitive, vision of the Divine Essence. Certainly the context suggests this interpretation, even if it does not demand it. Augustine wished to come into contact with God himself, alone, without any intermediary--*ipsum sine his audiamus*. And the immediate transition from the blissful vision at Ostia to the beatific vision of Heaven, quite independent of this interpretation though it may be, contributes in no small way to justify it. The assimilation of the one vision into the other is clearly indicated in the text. *Si continuetur hoc,* remarks Augustine, "let us suppose that this moment of delight, this intimate and immediate contact with God were to continue, that everything else were to disappear in the light of this all-absorbing encounter, would this not truly be the *gaudium Domini,* the enter into the joy of Your Lord, the realization of the future happiness which the Apostle foretold for the day of Resurrection?" Monica certainly shows that she understands Augustine's reflection in this sense, because she hastens to express her desire for heaven.

*

*   *

These are clearly the spontaneous impressions of the convert. His conceptions are not without limitations and will be modified as the years go by.

First, although the vision at Ostia took place shortly after Augustine's baptism, it is noteworthy that the actual version of the narrative that has come down to us was written several years later by a theologian who weighed his words and a bishop who was careful not to write anything that might expose him to criticism. In the introduction to his account, which pinpoints the meaning and was clearly written later, he explicitly states that in opening their souls to the heavenly stream of divine life, both mother and son were seeking to gain some idea of the eternal life of the saints. Thus, at the time of the *Confessions*, Augustine was certainly not afraid to admit that he had been seeking in his own experience, in this mystical ascent, a foretaste of heaven. And Augustine, who took great pains to correct all the errors of his youth in his *Retractationes*, made no change whatsoever in this passage.

For Augustine, eternal life is simply the vision at Ostia without end. Yet the formal characteristics of this vision are exactly the same as those of the highest Plotinian contemplation; for God himself is the object of knowledge and the specific mode of this knowledge is the vision of God in himself and by himself without any intermediary.[1] Here the object of contemplation is likewise the One, the Absolute of Plotinus, and no created form comes between the soul and Him. Moreover, the affective and mystical quality of the vision at Ostia is rarely absent from the *Enneads* and is particularly prominent in those treatises which were, at this time, a source of inspiration for Augustine. Thus, from the period of the *Confessions*, the formal characteristics and even the mystical tendencies of Neoplatonic ecstasy serve as concrete and vital prototype of what Christian theology would later call the "beatific vision." Indeed, this very expression can be found in Plotinus' famous treatise *On the Beautiful*. Here Augustine read: μακαριος οφιν μακαριαν τεθεαμενος (*Enn.*, I, 6, 7)-- "happiness will consist in this blessed vision." Such a discovery has stirred the barely concealed joy and cunning insinuations of some critics, the silent scandal and genuine sadness of others, as if the question of whether Christian dogma is transcendent or totally dependent upon Neoplatonism should be decided on the basis of this remarkable verbal similarity. Such critics view "beatific vision" as a mere translation of "blessed vision" from the *Enneads*, because as we see in the monumental *Thesaurus linguae latinae, beatificus* is rather rare in Latin before Augustine. And we must admit a doctrinal as well as a verbal similarity. But on the basis of such evidence are we willing to say that the author of the *Confessions*, even though a bishop, merely repeated the opinions of a neophyte inadequately instructed in the faith; are we willing to maintain that Augustine advanced his opinion as a matter for discussion and did not opt for one side or the other; or will we give up the case, resort to the final question mark of the dialogue at Ostia, and insist that the whole matter remain in doubt? All such approaches are subterfuges: they try to evade rather than resolve the issue and postpone its solution.

Turn to the *City of God*, that monument of doctrine and erudition which was twelve years in composition. We cannot say of this work, as we might of the *Confessions*, that it was written in haste, without concern for theology, and to unburden the heart. Plotinus' treatise *On the Beautiful* is cited twice, both times in books devoted to the problem of human destiny, and the quoted expression ends Plotinus' sentence which contains the term "blessed vision." More importantly, Augustine's text describing the beatific vision reveals a much closer doctrinal than verbal similarity to the passage from the *Enneads* which was one of the sources of the contemplation at Milan and vision at Ostia. Augustine's very question leads us to the heart of the matter and obviates all confusion. He writes: "Therefore, what angel should we trust on the subject of eternal life and beatitude--*sempiterna vita*? [The very expression used in the vision at Ostia.] Do not some claim religious worship for themselves, demanding divine honors for mortals; and do not others refer these honors to the Creator of the Universe, and insist that true piety will lead them to this God, *to the one God whose vision constitutes their beatitude, and who promises us that this beatitude will be ours*?" Each word is important. The blessed enjoy the same beatitude as the angels. But what, according to Augustine, is this common beatitude in this common vision? He continues: "For this vision is so sublimely beautiful and worthy of such great love that Plotinus does not hesitate to state that if a man is without it, even though he abounds in all other goods, he is utterly miserable" (*Civ.*, X, xvi). Describing the vision of the One, Plotinus had written: "Here the greatest and supreme struggle is imposed upon the soul and she must direct all her energy to it in order that she may not be without a share in the noblest of visions; he who attains it is happy because of this blessed vision; he who does not attain it is utterly miserable" (*Enn.*, I, 6, 7). As we know, this text numbers among those which played a part in Augustine's conversion and in his first mystical contemplations.

Some may claim that such an interpretation exaggerates the importance of an isolated text, a passing remark, that the bishop would never have compared the natural and philosophical "noblest of visions" sought by Plotinus with the beatific vision, the ultimate supernatural end of angels and men. In point of fact he did and the amazing comparison was not inadvertent.

At the end of Book X of the *City of God*, a section concerned with final beatitude, Augustine asserts that our happiness is the same as that of the celestial spirits and then goes on to complete his thought on the subject. Cited in its entirety, this page will clarify the issue. The first sentence is extremely concise and clear. Referring to the Platonists, Augustine writes: "But we have no dispute with these celebrated philosophers on this question. For they have seen and have continually proven in their writings that our happiness and that of these immortal spirits flows from the same source." Augustine proceeds to describe it: "They are diffused with an intelligible light which is their God and is distinct from them. His ray enlightens them and an intimate possession of Him is the condition of their perfection and beatitude." Once again the treatises of Plotinus make an appearance, particularly the treatise *On the Three Hypostases*, the principal philosophical source of the vision at Ostia. The text continues: "Commenting on Plato, Plotinus continually asserts that this very soul, which he considers the universal soul, derives its happiness from the same source as we derive ours; that this principal, which is distinct from it, gives it being and illumines it with an intelligible ray, and thus makes it shine with an intelligible clarity. . . ." In the following passage, notice first the parenthesis which has some bearing on our subject, and second the absence of an intermediary in the vision. "Thus this great Platonist maintains that the rational soul, or rather the intellectual soul (for under this name it also includes the souls of the blessed immortal beings whom he places in heaven), that this intellectual soul indeed knows no nature above itself, and that these heavenly spirits receive their beatitude and the light of understanding and truth from the same source as we ourselves receive them." Augustine confidently concludes that, "This doctrine is in accord with these words of the Gospel: 'There was a man sent from God whose name was John. He came as a witness to give testimony concerning the Light, that all might believe through him. He was not himself the Light but came to bear witness to the Light, the true Light that enlightens every man who comes into the world.' This distinction shows clearly enough," continues Augustine, "that the rational or intellectual soul, as found in

St. John, cannot illuminate itself and that it enlightens only through participation in the true Light. And John himself gives testimony concerning this Light when he says that, 'Of His fulness we have all received'" (*Civ.*, X, ii).

It would be foolish to maintain that Augustine did not tamper with Plotinus' thought throughout this passage in order to make it agree more perfectly with the thought of the Church. Here, where he is treating of eternal beatitude, as in the ecstasy at Ostia, the role of the Word in the vision of God is heavily accented. When we consider that for Plotinus the Intelligence, the second hypostasis of the *Enneads*, is certainly not the Absolute, while for the Christian theologian the Word, the equal of the Father, is God, the care Augustine took to bring these two positions into harmony becomes all the more obvious. The parallel between the Johannine Prologue and the *Enneads* shows clearly enough that the synthesis of dogma and philosophy realized at Milan, most particularly on the doctrine of the Word, did not weaken but grew more solid as the years passed.

In a curious text dealing with the Trinity, the end of man which consists in contemplation of the Triune God, and the Incarnation which is the way to beatitude, Augustine makes some astonishing concessions to Porphyry.

> You acknowledge the Father and the Son, whom you call the understanding of the Father, and a being who is an intermediary between them, whom you present, I believe, as the Holy Spirit. Thus, in spite of the freedom of your language and of an uncertain and partially clouded vision, you still perceive the end towards which we must strive, but you are unwilling to acknowledge the Incarnation of the immutable Son of God, a mystery of our salvation which raises us towards the object of our faith and which our understanding grasps only with difficulty.

> You perceive the region of the fatherland in a distance and as if through a cloud, but you do not stay on the road that must be followed.
>
> *Civ.*, X, xxix

The last sentence almost sounds like an echo of the *Confessions*.

Where, then, is there any indication that the mature Augustine rejected the Platonic notions concerning the *Logos* which had attracted him in his youth? Indeed the *De civitate Dei* very often seems merely to express in more abstract terms certain convictions formed during the critical years described in Augustine's autobiography. This is quite evident in his treatment of the nature of the beatific vision, as the previously cited texts clearly prove.

This continuity of thought is also evident from the whole scheme of the work. In Book XIX of the *City of God*, Augustine enumerates the philosophical sects which led him into error on the question of the sovereign good. The Neoplatonists are not mentioned. This silence is eloquent; for the only passages in which they are mentioned introduce them as favorable witnesses of the Christian conception of beatitude. In the final Book of the work, probably one of the most carefully composed and most important, Augustine paints a majestic picture of heaven, the *City of God* in its ultimate perfection. He devotes only a few lines to the Neoplatonists, but these lines are pregnant with meaning. "The celebrated philosophers do not differ from our opinion of the rewards which the blessed soul is to enjoy in the afterlife; it is the resurrection of the body that they contest and strenuously deny" (*Civ.*, XXII, xxv). Disagreement on this second point accentuates the fundamental agreement on the first, on the essence of eternal beatitude which for a Christian, as the author had said earlier, can be nothing other than the face-to-face vision of God.

How is such agreement possible? How can a bishop admit that a pagan philosopher can arrive at a conception of beatitude which is like that of Christian theology and which seems to be reserved to it alone? If by unaided natural powers Plotinus can attain or can even conceive of the supernatural end which revelation promises the Christian through the merits of Jesus Christ, the transcendence of dogma would seem to be endangered. Such an objection can be answered by a fact and, because the difficulty is partially theological, by a doctrine of faith. We must not forget that Plotinus lived in the third century after Jesus Christ, that for twenty years he taught in Rome, the very heart of Christianity, and while there, as well as at Alexandria, he could have become acquainted with the content of Christian revelation. Or else, if this sublime conception of the vision of God appears to be the spontaneous product and, as it were, the flowering of the last branch of Greek philosophy, does not Christian theology maintain that the sun of grace shines upon all men and that, whether they wish it or not, whether they are conscious of it or not, they live and die in the shadow of the redemptive cross?

Augustine had either heard or foreseen this objection. He answered: "Some of our brothers in the grace of Jesus Christ are amazed to learn, whether through conversation or reading, that Plato had ideas of God which they recognize as remarkably similar to the truths of our religion" (*Civ.*, VIII, xi). We might add that such similarity is even more obvious in Plotinus. And after Augustine realized that he could not be sure that these philosophers had been familiar with the holy books, as he had first thought, he concluded: "But from whatever source he derived these truths, whether from the works of antiquity (this initial response is not entirely satisfactory) or whether, as seems more likely, from the light which, according to the words of the Apostle, 'has manifested to them what can be known of God through natural means, that is, God himself has revealed this to them; for since the creation of the world, the eye of the understanding has seen mirrored in what He has made, the invisible nature of God, His eternal power and divinity'; I purposely chose the Platonists over all other philosophers for the discussion of the following question of natural theology: whether or not we must serve one God or many if we are to obtain the happiness of the afterlife" (*Civ.*, VIII, xii). Once again, the discussion is not about the very end of man or about the nature of beatitude, but about the means which should lead us to it.

If we are to enter our celestial fatherland, if we are to see God as He is in Himself, must we call upon the many gods of Paganism or the single Mediator, Jesus Christ? The *Confessions* have already shown us that faith in the Incarnation distinguishes the Plotinian doctrine of destiny from the Christian dogma of salvation. This faith, which is totally absent from the *Enneads*, is the basis of Augustine's whole theology: *ibi legi. . . .ibi non legi.* The same theme is taken up again in the *City of God* in a more developed but no less moving form, and thus we have a further proof of the continuity between the convert's first impressions and the Doctor's mature opinions.

> The happiness of the blessed multitude consists only in being united with a single God; the miserable multitude of bad angels, being deprived of this union, rises up to hinder us rather than to come to our aid: it is a malevolent swarm which drones around us, so to speak, in order to turn us from the path of this sovereign beatitude which is calling us, we do not need many mediators but only one, that Mediator in union with whom we become happy, the Word of God, the uncreated Word, creator of all things. Yet He is not Mediator inasmuch as He is the Word;

> for the Word is far removed from miserable mortals in the lofty realm of his eternity and glory, but He is Mediator inasmuch as He is man.
>
> In this way, He shows us that to reach the God who possesses and grants beatitude, we need not seek other mediators to provide the steps for us, because the God from whom all beatitude flows has given us ready access to his divinity in deigning to share our humanity. In delivering us from mortality and misery, He does not unite us with the angels that we might become immortal by their immortality and blessed by their beatitude; He elevates us even to the very Trinity in communion with whom the angels are blessed. Thus, while in order to become Mediator He wills to be lower than the angels, taking the form of a slave, He still remains above the angels according to His divine nature; He who is life itself in heaven is the way of life here on earth.
>
> *Civ.*, IX, xv

This passage contains an echo, magnified and resounding through a whole theology, of Augustine's beliefs and aspirations as he returned to God, beliefs and aspirations already noted throughout the *Confessions*.

The Christian Doctor still qualified and amended the Neoplatonic theory of beatitude. Even though the two thinkers agree on the end to be attained, nevertheless the proud pretensions of Plotinus seemed vain to Augustine: man will never reach this "excellent contemplation" of the divinity through his own power. And even when he does attain it in this life through a grace from on high, "a quite extraordinary and very rare occurrence" (*Civ.*, XI, ii) he does not experience perfect happiness, reflected the bishop in terms so similar to those of the vision at Ostia that he may well have had it in mind. For here below, all such visions, no matter how sublime they may be, are only momentary--*momentum intellegentiae*--and in order to produce perfect happiness--*gaudium Domini*--they must, as we read in the *Confessions*, be free of error and illusion and must continue forever--*si continuetur hoc*. In the *City of God*, the author clearly insists upon this twofold condition: "This state will be eternal and we will be assured of its eternity, and our supreme good will consist in this" (*Civ.*, XIX, xxvii).

Throughout the course of his long Christian career, St. Augustine neither added to nor subtracted from his teaching on this point. Insofar as the Neoplatonists placed the essence of beatitude in the intuitive and immediate vision of God, he considered their opinion correct. But insofar as they thought that they could attain such beatitude here below, and above all without grace, without the one and only Mediator between God and men, without Jesus Christ, they were grossly deceived. This difference of opinion, an important corollary to the dogma of the Incarnation, is expressed magnificently in the *Confessions:* "It is one thing to see the land of peace from the wooded summit, without finding the path which leads to it, and to struggle hopelessly through the wayless tracts along with fugitives and deserters; it is quite another to remain on the path that will lead there, a path guarded by the solicitude of the heavenly Prince. . ." (*Conf.*, VII, 27). But both the author of the *Enneads* and the author of the *Confessions* and *City of God* wished to hasten to the same fatherland where the Father awaited them--*ibi pater et ibi omnia*. Augustine saw that Plotinus had fallen into error, but they were not in total disagreement

Some of the essential characteristics of the blessed vision of Plotinus are contained in the vision at Ostia where, by a sort of montage, one vision is superimposed upon the other. Experience directed the intellectual synthesis of dogma and philosophy. If, on the one hand, the Augustinian conception of beatitude underwent noticeable development from the time of the contemplation at Milan and the *Dialogues* of Cassiciacum until the ecstasy at Ostia and the narrative of the *Confessions*--and this is noted in the *Retractationes*--on the other hand, it suffered no profound alteration from the time of the *Confessions* until the *City of God*. It was originally embodied in a concrete psychological state, but thereafter developed only in theological formulae. Even the most subtle aspects of the bishop's doctrine were present in the neophyte's mystical experience. Before baptism, religion seemed largely a matter of dogma and a criterion of certitude; thereafter it did not cease to be such, but it also became a way of life and a guarantee of happiness. As a hugh wave which washes the soft sands of the shore, catholicism invaded the convert's whole soul and supplied needed faith, vision, and love. Nothing escaped it, and yet it respected everything; it glided into every nook and cranny, not on a mission of destruction, but in order to raise everything above its natural level by a gentle and irresistible swell. In the vision at Ostia, this rising tide reached its peak for an instant, then the ebb carried it away. But from this moment on, Augustine would look upon religion as a source of revelation, a system of thought, and a way of life. If the mystical element was most prominent, it was because the attraction of the end exerted a greater influence, and because it was more in accord with the demands of the *fecisti nos ad te*, that spontaneous cry from the depths of Augustine's soul. This soul's total experience entered into the doctrine of the Church.

As the vision at Ostia, recounted in the last book of a personal history, integrated the three elements of all earthly religion, so the beatific vision, of which the vision at Ostia was a prelude and model and which is described on the closing page of a universal history, will also preserve something of the three essential elements of Christianity here below. Thus Augustine concludes the *City of God* with a description of heaven: "There we shall be at rest and we shall see, we shall see and we shall love, we shall love and we shall praise--*Ibi vacabimus et videbimus, videbimus et amabimus, amabimus et laudabimus*. We shall see; for we shall be suffused with light in the truth of the Word. We shall love; for through the action of the Spirit we shall possess God within ourselves. The life of grace will become the light of glory for the intellect and heart, a light that is without shadow and yet still mysterious. Certainly hope will be fulfilled--*vacabimus*--faith will vanish--*videbimus*--love will be full--*amabimus*. But in addition to the total gift of self in charity, that charity which remains, there will still be an analogical basis for faith and hope: the acceptance of a transcendent object, something of a respectful, submissive desire to possess it more perfectly, and exultant joy in the incomprehensible excellence of this object--*laudabimus*.

Where all is perfectly clear, adoration is impossible. But the finitude of the created being will still be an obstacle to the total comprehension of the Infinite. Man's intellect will still be inadequate for the divine reality and, in heaven as on earth, humility will still be the primary virtue. The new religion, which Christ revealed to the Samaritan woman at the well of Jacob and which Augustine made completely his own in "a supreme burst of love" during the vision at Ostia, will endure eternally and in its entirety in the beatific vision: in heaven face to face as on earth through faith, the Christian will still be able and will still be obliged to adore God in spirit and in truth.

NOTES

1. It has even been noted that there is no explicit mention of the Trinity in the vision at Ostia.